Gandhian Studies and Peace Research Series No. 14

GANDHIAN SATYAGRAHA

An Analytical and Critical Approach

DR. AJAY SHANKER RAI
M.A., B.Ed., L.L.B., Ph.D.
(Sahityalankar)

CONCEPT PUBLISHING COMPANY, NEW DELHI-110059

ISBN: 81-7022-799-2

First Published 2000

Published and Printed by
Ashok Kumar Mittal
Concept Publishing Company
A/15-16, Commercial Block, Mohan Garden,
New Delhi-110059

Phones : 5648039, 5649024
Fax : 091-11-5648053

GANDHIAN SATYAGRAHA
An Analytical and Critical Apporoach

GANDHIAN STUDIES AND PEACE RESEARCH SERIES (GSPRS)

1. Gandhian Model of Development and World Peace, *R.P. Misra*
2. Conflict Resolution Through Non-Violence : Role of the Universities, Vol. I: Science and Ethics, *K.D. Gangrade* and *R.P. Misra*
3. Conflict Resolution Through Non-Violence : Role of Universities, Vol. II : Development Without Destruction, *K.D. Gangrade* and *R.P. Misra*
4. The Social Philosophy of Mahatma Gandhi, *K.S. Bharathi*
5. Gandhian Humanism, *Mohit Chakrabarty*
6. Gandhian Holistic Economics, *Shashi Prabha Sharma*
7. Gandhian Spiritualism : A Quest for the Essence of Excellence, *Mohit Chakrabarty.*
8. Gandhian Perspective on Population and Development, *A.K. Sharma*
9. Thoughts of Gandhi and Vinoba : A Comparative Study, *K.S. Bharathi*
10. Economic Philosophy of Mahatma Gandhi, *Shanti Swarup Gupta*
11. The Political Thoughts of Mahatma Gandhi, *K.S. Bharathi.*
12. Gandhi and 21st Century, *Janardan Pandey* (Ed.)
13. Gandhian Philosophy of the Spinning Wheel, *Mohit Chakrabarty*
14. Gandhian Satyagraha : An Analytical and Critical Approach, *Ajay Shankar Rai*

About the Author

Dr. Ajay Shankar Rai, is Lecturer, (Specialisation in Indian Philosophy) in Department of Philosophy S.S.M. College, Chitra, Deoghar since 1993. He took his B.A. (Hons) in 1988, M.A. in 1991, B.Ed in 1992 from Patna University. He took Sahityalankar in the year 1994 from Hindi Vidyapith Deoghar, L.L.B. from Bhagalpur University in the year 1996. He obtained his Ph. D. from Patna University in the year 1998.

Dr. Rai has been actively engaged in writing books and articles. He is working on social philosophy, Radical Humanism and Indian Philosophy.

PREFACE

This book *Gandhian Satyagraha: An Analytical and Critical Approach* apparently indicates that Gandhi is not consistent with his views on Satyagraha, a technique of non-violent political movement. Gandhi confidently implies it in the field of Socio-Political arena, though he has better experiences of its practical implications. I have made an attempt to show the cause of bitterness of Satyagraha experienced not by Gandhi but by ourselves too. This practical bitterness depends on the contradictions inhert in *Satyagraha*.

Before analysing and finding out the contradictions of *Satyagraha*, it is essential to brief a short sketch of Mahatma Gandhi's life and works. So I have started with the brief introduction of Gandhi's life and works. Then I have attempted to find out the meaning and sources of Satyagraha. Satyagraha as a moral theory is traced out in different testimonies like *Vedas, Upnisada, Geeta, Mahabharata, Ramayana* etc. After tracing out the source of Satyagraha, I have analysed elements and forms of Satyagraha. God, truth, non-violence etc. are elements of Satyagraha. Civil disobedience, non-cooperation, fasting etc. are forms of Satyagraha. In course of analysis of elements and forms, I have searched out contradictions invariably lain inherent in them. It proves that Satyagraha itself is full of contradictions. A contradictory theory always reflects on the society negatively. Therefore, I conclude my thesis in establishing the negative implication of Satyagraha in our society. The work is originally a thesis for Ph. D. degree is now published with some modifications and additions. I feel that it is a herculean task which cannot be fulfilled without the help of my esteemed teacher and supervisor, Dr. N. P. Tiwary, Reader, Department of Philosophy, B. N. College, Patna University Patna. Therefore, I am extreemly indebted in recording my deep sense of gratitude to him for his encouragement, inspiration, sympathetic attitude, valuable guidance and advise during the completion of this work.

'Aarti Bhawan'
Court Road,
Deoghar (Bihar)

AJAY SHANKER RAI

CONTENTS

INTRODUCTION

The twentieth century which has a little more than a decade to complete itself has produced many outstanding Socio-Political leaders and reformers. Among them Mahatma Gandhi achieved a universal name. Mahatma Gandhi, whose life is a living record of varieties of experiences during his stay in these three continents—Asia, Europe and Africa was born on 2nd October 1869 at Porbandar in Kathiawad the small north western land which forms one of the State of Gujarat. His father's name was Karamchand and mother's Putlibai. He belonged to the Vaishya Baniya or trading the third of the four *varnas* of Hinduism. Gandhi spended his childhood in Porbandar. His family followed the theistic faith Vaisnavism. He was born and nursed in such an atmosphere where worshipping God, taking sacred vows and fastings were usual practices in his family. His father was true and loyal sarvent and member of the court in Porbandar. His mother Putlibai left an outstanding impression of her saintliness. She was deeply religious. She was regular practioner of *Chaturmas.** She used to take the hardest vows and kept them without flinching. Mahatma Gandhi grew in such a mixed and ballanced setup. He was the result of such an atmosphere and infact he was real offspring of his real ancesstors. He received his own real investments from his ancesstors and forefathers. The environment and atmosphere of his family played a crucial role upon the growth and all round development of Mahatma Gandhi. His mother and nurse were particularly devotee and he followed their faith and got current sacred names.

Gandhi spent his childhood in Porbandar. Afterwards his father left Porbandar and came to Rajkot becoming a member of the Rajasthanik Court. Here Gandhi got his primary education in a school being a mediocre student. From here Gandhi went to the suburban

* *Chaturmas :* A period of four months when fasting and semi fasting takes place. It is a period of long lent.

school. At the age of twelve he became a student of High School. At school stage he never told a lie. He was very shy natured and avoided company of all. His books and lessons were his sole companions. His soul was such a good and true one that one's at high school examination he was brought into notice that he refused to copy in the examination. He never learnt the art of copying because he was against copying. He only learnt to carry the words and orders of elders and not to scan their actions, because he was by nature blind to the faults of the elders.

Mahatma Gandhi was married to Kasturba at the early age of thirteen, when he was a student in school. His wife was illiterate and by nature simple, independent, preserving and reticent. In those days separation was unbearable. "I used to keep her awake till late in the night with my idle talk. If with this passion there had not been in me a burning attachment to duty, I should either have fallen a prey to disease and premature death or have sank into a burdensome existence", said Gandhi, "The tasks was this last thing that saved me from many a pitfal".[1] Gandhi was learning at high school when he lost his father 1885. But he continued his studies inspite of his marriage and father's death. He disliked both gymnastics and cricket from very childhood. His shyness was one of the reason for this aloofness. He had the notion at that early stage that games and sports have nothing to do with education. He developed a habit of taking walks which remained with him untill death.. The reason of dislike for these games was his keen desire to serve his father.

Gandhi had a distaste for any reading beyond his school books. But at very school stage he was much impressed by a book *'Shravana Pitribhakti'*. This book left such an impact upon his mind, how Shravana carried his blind parents on his shoulders on a pilgrimage, that remained in his mind and heart uptill death. Just about this same time Gandhi was touched to deep of his heart by a play Harishchandra, which captured his heart and rose a question in his mind day and night, 'Why should not all be truthfull like Harischandra ?' To follow truth and to go through all the ordeals Harischandra went through was the one ideal which inspired in him. For him uptill his death Harischandra and Sravana were not a historical character but remained living realities.

At the high school Gandhi made friends who were originally friends of his elder brother's. This friendship proved a tragedy in the life of Mahatma Gandhi. His desire was to reform his friends removing their weakness and to made them a splendid man. But later his calculation proved wrong because a reformer cannot afford to have close intimacy with him whom he seeks to reform. He decided to avoid all exclusive intimacies and to be friend with God only or make the whole world his friend. This decision turned the whole life of Gandhi to its each and every aspect.

Inspired by his friends and effect of a doggerel of the Gujrati poet Narmad,

> Behold the might Englishman
> He rules the Indian small
> Because being a meat eater
> He is five cubits tall.

He started believing that meat eating was good and if whole country took to meat eating, the English could be overpowered. Being and off spring of staunch Vaishnavas his love of truth made him extra cautious and as a result he was bent on the reform. The frenzy of the reform blinded him and he decided even to deceive his parents. He persuaded himself that mere hiding the deed from parents was no departure from truth. He started meat eating and had taken meat dishes several times as a reform on his own part. Dinner at home was out of question and he used to lie with his mother. "I knew I was lying and lying to my mother. I also knew that if my mother and father came to know of my having become a meat eater they would be deeply shocked".[2] This knowledge gnawened his heart. This turned Gandhi towards truth and he said, "though it is essential to eat meat, and also to take up food reform in the country, yet deceiving and lying to one's father and mother is worse than not eating meat".[3] Then Gandhi took a vow that "When they are no more and I have found my freedom, I will eat meat openly, but untill that moment arrives I will abstain from it".[4] After this incident Gandhi never went back to take meat and remained vegetarian for whole life.

In his early age Gandhi fell prey to the bad habit of smoking. He was simply getting pleasure in emitting clouds of smoke from his mouth. He used to smoke pilfering stumps of cigarattes thrown away by uncle. In absence of stumps and cigarattes Gandhi used to steal coppers from the pocket of his elders. Due to the hard gurdianship he once decided to commit suicide, but later he realised his fault and contemplated it. This thought of suicide resulted in making good bye to the habit of smoking and stealing. But the real greatness of the child Mohan Das was that realising his guilty he made a confession to his father by writing it on a slip of paper. He not only confessed but also asked for adequate punishment for his guilty pleading not to do such one again. This reveals that the greatness was inherent in Gandhi from his very childhood. Gandhi himself said in his autobiography that this was for me an object - lesson in *Ahinsa*. Then I could read in it nothing more than father's love who forgave me, but today I know that it was pure ahinsa. When such ahinsa becomes all embrassing it transforms everything it touches. There is not limit to this power.[5]

When Gandhi was at the age of sixteen as a student in high school he lost his father, he continued his studies and passed his matriculation examination in 1887. Then he joined a college at Bhavanagar. But he found himself entirely at a sea and later discontinuing his college studies returned his home. At that time a shrewd and learned Brahman, an old friend and adviser of his family Mavji Dave advised to go England and become a barrister.

Gandhi accepted the proposal but he was interested in medical profession, but due to disfavour his brother and dislikeness of late father for medical profession, Gandhi decided to become a barrister. Becharji Swami, a jain monk administered not to touch wine, women and meat. After taking permission of his mother, taking the solemn vows in her pressure, he sailed to Southampton in England with a Junagadh Vakil on the 4th of September 1888. This vow, his love and regard taken at the early stage in regard to his mother pushed and pulled him up from the brink of temptation. These all made such an impact upon him that it made him a man taking vows on several occasions for his pious wishes effective, and thus he started testifying the efficacy of vows as tought by Hindu and Jaina thoughts from his own life.

In England Gandhi diligently learned all the great and good things of the West. He never provided much attention to his legel studies. He pursuaded mostly towards diverse paths of interests. He used to spent a large part of his time cultivating acquaintance through books, meetings and discussions with several moral, religious and dietetic movements of the West. He gained deep knowledge and confidence in the things that are great in the Indian culture. He had never read a newspaper in India, but in England he succeeded in cultivating a liking for newspaper by regular reading and taking a glance over *The Daily News, The Daily Telegraph* and *The Pall Mall Gassette.*

Gandhi once launched out in search of a vegetarian restaurant and found it at Farringdon Street. Here he saw Salt's plea for vegetarianism. This was his first hearty meal since his arrival in England. Gandhi went through the Salt's book from cover to cover and claimed to have become a vegetarian by choice. This book left a lasting impression upon the mind and heart of Gandhi and from that very day he decided to spread the dietetic movement in favour of vegetarianism through out the world. His faith in vegetarianism grew day by day and his appetite for dietetic studies rose the plea for vegetarianism to its greatest extent. He went through all books available on vegetarianism like Howard Williams' *The Ethics of Diet*, Dr. Anna Kingsford's *The Perfect way in Diet*. Dr. Allinson's writings on health and hygiene which all proved helpful to him. The result of reading all these literatures was the dietetic experiments took an important place in his life. Health was the principal consideration of Gandhi's dietetic experiments but later on religion became the supreme goal.

Gandhi was so much concious that the infatuation with English system lasted nearly for three months and hence he became a student. But these period of infatuation gave him a certain amount of self introspection. As a result he became such a Calculative person that he got entered every little item. He used to keep account of every farthing he spent and this habit stayed with him ever since whole of his life. He always kept a strict watch over his way of living and this plain living saved plenty of time and money which helped him in passing his London Matriculation. This fulfilled his satisfaction of taking a difficult examination, and this change harmonized his outward and inward life. He attained a complete change in his both internal and external life. He came accross all kinds of vegetarian's and lastly join a vegetarian society in England which had a weekly journal of its own. Gandhi subscribed to the weekly and in a short period became a Chair person in the executive committee. Here he made his own experiments in dietetics. "Such experiments tought me that real seat of taste was not the tongue but the mind".[6] The experiment conducted in England were from the point of view of with economy and hygiene. Vegetarianism was at that time a new cult in England and Gandhi moved a step ahead by starting a vegetarian club in his own locality. Dr. Oldfield, who was the editor of "The Vegetarian" became president and Sir Edwin Arnold became the Vice-President. Gandhi himself became the secretary of the club.

Going through his legel studies Gandhi came to know a couple of great things. Firstly, he came to know the maxim that the two-third of the law are facts. Secondly, he got such an abiding impressing from legel principles that resulted in his theory of trusteeship. He adopted these two maxims in his legal and socio-political work because it fitted perfectly in his ideas and respect of truth. These developed the habit of living economically and keeping daily accounts of his expenses. All the basic principles of Gandhi were set up and habits were formed by the time he left England. He was inclined to a life which according to him was the best, the world has produced through its greatest men and the life on which the East and the West could meet. In England for the first time he discovered the futility of mere religious knowledge after going through different Secred Books. In 1890 Gandhi also attain a vegetarian conference at Portsmouth in England. Here in Portsmouth he came to know about invisible power or divine power 'God', when he was saved from going beyond the limit, with unknown woman. He says that, "God warned me through the good Companion"[7]. After this incident he understood the God in the help of the helpless and the strength of the weak. In the same year 1890 Gandhi went to Paris to see a great exhibition. He stayed there for seven days and travelled Paris from one end to another. About Eiffel Tower he said what Tolstoy had told earlier that the Eiffel Tower is a monument of man's folly, not of his wisdom.

Along with all extra activities Gandhi was serious to his legal studies. He went through Broom's 'Common Law', Snell's 'Equity', Tudor's 'Leading Cases' and William's and Edward's 'Real Property'.

He also read Goodeve's *Personal Property*, which was like a noval. After an honest and devoted study Gandhi passed his legal studies examination and was called to the Bar on the 10th of June 1891. He enrolled himself in the High Court on the 11th. But after becoming barriser-in-law he sailed for India back to home on 12th June 1891.

Gandhi started a household with a cook in Bombay. Here in Bombay he started the study of Indian Law. On the other hand he continued his experiments in dietetics with help of a friend Virchand Gandhi. For him the study of Indian Law was a tedious business. He was not serious to his studies and went through the Evidence Act and Mayne's Hindu Law. But he had not courage to conduct the case. The very first case as a barrister was Mamibai's Case. Soon he found himself unable to stay in Bombay. "I found the barrister's profession a bad job of much show and little knowledge".[8] Finding himself unable to follow cases he decided to settle in Rajkot where his brother was a petty pleader. He closed his little establishment in Bombay after a stay of six months. He attended High Court in Bombay and said,"I cannot say that I learnt anything there".[9]

At that time Porbandar was under administration and Gandhi did there work.to secure much powers for the prince.

Also he was to see the administrator in respect of land revenue. At that time he found an offer from Meman from Porbandar to go to South Africa for a big case. It was hardly going there as a barrister, but as a servent of the firm. Gandhi was tempted to see a new country and also wanted to leave India for some new experience. Through Dada Abdulla and Company in April 1893 Gandhi sailed for South Africa to work in the case with full of zest to try his luck there. He reached the Port of Natal in Durban towards the close of May. Abdulla Sheth received him and took him to the firm's place. He went to see the Durban Court and was shocked finding a clear distinction between Muslims and other Indians. Except Muslims, none of the Indians were allowed to keep their turbans. He also found that Indians were divided into different groups. He was called a 'Coolie Barrister", because the word *coolie* was a common appellation for all Indians in South Africa. Here he got an unexpected popularity within a few days because he wrote to the press about the incident and defended the wearing of party turban in the court. This turban stayed with him practically untill the end of his stay in South Africa.

Gandhi started the study the case from its ABC. He also went to Zanzibar to see the work in the court there. Then after few days he left Durben for Pretoria. When he was travelling in first class he was pulled down out of the train along with his luggage at Maritzburg because those days in South Africa coloured men were not allowed to travell in the first class. Inspite of his refusal he was pulled out by the constable. This very incident proved a milestone in Gandhi's life too much far extent which changed the whole life. He was compelled to think about the hardship to which he was subjected, only a symptom of the disease of colour prejudice. A question rose in his mind, either to fight for the rights or back to India without minding the insults. After a long ups and downs in mind, Gandhi went to Pretoria by the next available train.

Another incident which gave a set back to him was that after train journey he purchased a ticket for the coach for Johensburg, but the agent of the coach refused to accommodate inside the coach because he was regarded as a *coolie.* On many a humble request he was given seat next to the coachman which was sheer injustice. From Pardekoph, Gandhi went to Pretoria travelling in a first class compartment dressing himself in faultless English dress. Here in Pretoria he found the attorney Mr. A. W. Baker, who was completely free from colour prejudice. Here Gandhi came in contact with several Christian peoples. But he was desirous to come in contact with Indians. So he called a meeting of all Indians in Pretoria and presented a picture before them of the condition of Indian peoples in South Africa. It was the first public speech in a public meeting in life of Mahatma Gandhi. He made a deep study of Social, Political and Economic condition of Indians in Pretoria. This study proved invaluable for Gandhi in the future because here he learnt the success as a lawyer. He knew the true practice of law. He realized that the true function of a lawyer is to unite the different parties.

After the case was concluded, Gandhi returned back to Durban and decided to return home. But it was proved that nothing happens according to one's own will. Knowing about the Indian Franchise Bill he was shocked because he found that the bill was to strike at the root of self respect of Indians. People decided to go against the bill in the court and in this course they asked Gandhi to stay in Durban for the same. Thus the farewell party which was given in honour of Gandhi turned into a working committee and this was the foundation of life in South Africa and sowed the seed of the fight for national self respect. Gandhi settled in Natal and arranged several meetings of Indians. He went through all literatures available on the subject and his arguments was centred round a principle and an expedience. He got retainer for one year legal work of twenty merchants and it was impossible for him to leave Natal. He applied for admission as an advocate of the Supreme Court. But the Law Society opposed in saying that a coloured man cannot be allowed as an advocate in Supreme Court. Later after some time he gave affidavit of Sheth Abdulla to the Law Society. Again the Law Society opposed it before the Supreme Court, but the court ruled out the opposition and admitted the application of Gandhi. Here the practice as a lawyer remained a subordinate occupation. The opposition of the Law Society gave him much popularity in South Africa through the media.

After getting settled there, Gandhi found necessity of a sustained agitation, and for this purpose he decided to have a public organisation of a permanent character. After full explanation the Natal Indian Congress came into being on 22nd of May. He wrote two pamphlets—the first was "An Appeal to Every Indian in South Africa", and other was "The Indian Frenchise—An Appeal". All this activity resulted in winning the Indian freinds in South Africa. It in fact opened out and placed before the South African Indians a definite line of action.

After three years stay in South Africa Mahatma Gandhi decided to return home to fetch up his wife and children and again return to settle in South Africa. He sailed for India in the year 1896, landed at

Calcutta and arrived Bombay by train. In India he spended some time in going about the country to know his motherland. Afterwards he settled at Rajkot and started writing pamphlet on the condition of Indians in south Africa known as "Green Pamphlet". In it he drew the picture of the condition of Indians which was concluded with help of childrens as his co-workers. He also gave his service to the sanitation department when plague broke out in Maharashtra. By that time Gandhi's conception of *ahimsa* became much matured. On the occasion of king Edward VII's coronation as Emperor of India, the text was jarred on him. He was at that time more vigilant about his own thought and speech, which jarred upon his own sentiment of *Ahimsa.* He delivered a speech in Bombay in Sir Cowasji Jehangir Institute in accordence with Sir Pherozeshah's instructions. From Bombay he went to Poona where he met Lokamanya Tilak for the first time, who impressed him to a great extent. Next he met Gokhale, who won his heart. In words of Mahatma Gandhi, "Sir Pherozeshah had seemed to me like Himalayas, Lokamanya like the Ocean. But Gokhale was like the Ganges in which one could have a refreshing bath in a holy river. The Himalaya was unshakable and unscaleble, as one could not easily launch forth on the sea, but the Ganges invited one to its bosom. It was a joy to be on it with a boat and an oar."[10] Gokhale closely examined Gandhi as a school master and that in why Gokhale occupied absolutely unique place in the heart of Gandhi during his life time and afterwards in the sphere of politics.

From Poona Gandhi went to Madras with wild enthusiasm. Here he found sympathy and guidance of Sjt. G. Parameshvaran Pillay, the editor of *The Madras Standard* and Sjt G. Subrahmaniam of *The Hindu.* He was given the responsibility to dispose the columns of the Madras standard. He stayed at Madras along with his writings. But sooner he left for Calcutta where he became acquainted with Mr. Ellerthorpe, a representative of *The Daily Telegraph.*

Here he saw for the first time S.N. Banerjee, the Idol of Bengal. He met him and asked for help in his work, but Surendranath refused to do so. Then Gandhi met the Anglo Indian editor of *The Statesman* and *The Englishman*, who were impressed from Gandhi's work and personality. Mr. Sounders, editor of *The Englishman* placed his office and paper at his disposal. Than Gandhi decided to hold a meeting in Culcutta with help of Mr. Saunder. But in the mean time Gandhi received a cable from Durban to return soon to South Africa. In December 1896 Gandhi returned to South Africa with his wife, two sons and the only widow sister. They arrived Durban on the 18th or

19th of December. Between the period 1897 to 1899 Gandhi came straight to the Boer War. He saved the war affected people with help of an ambulance corps. His loyality to the British drove him to participate with the British in that war. During this war for the first time Gandhi became thoughtful for India's freedom. He thought that India could achieve her complete emancipation only within and through the British Empire. This was the very first occasion when Gandhi thought about Indian's freedom. Here we can say that the seed of the freedom movement leaded by Gandhi for India had been long sown. It only needed watering to take root, to flower and to fruitify which all came in due course. "The service of the Indians in South Africa revealed to me new implications of truth at every stage".[11]

Again in the year 1899 Mahatma Gandhi returned to India. This time he had some keen desire to know his motherland going in her lap, to know her in her wholeness. In the year 1901 Congress met at Calcutta which was also attended by Gandhi. This was his very first experience of Indian Congress. He offered his service to the Congress office to gain experience working as a clerk and a bearer in the Congress Office. He in this Congress session met several leaders and specially observed them. He came in contact with the movements of stalwarts like Surendranath and Gokhale and spended near about a month with Gokhale. In his stay at Calcutta he walked ups and downs of the streets in Calcutta. He used to divide his whole day between seeing the leading people in Calcutta regarding the work in South Africa, and visiting for the study of the religious and public institutions of the city. Here he once addressed a meeting presided by Dr. Mullick on the work of the Indian corps in South African Boer War. Gokhale praised his speech and at this time under the roof of Gokhale he came in touch with the foremost Bengali families. This was the beginning of Gandhi's intimate contact with Bengal. He also visited Burma and the Burmese Monks. On his return from Burma Gandhi went to Rajkot after taking leave from Gokhale. Though Gokhale advised him to settle in Bombay to practice as a barrister and help in the work of the Congress, overconfident of his success as a barrister, Gandhi started his work at Rajkot with help of Kevalram Mavji Dave. Later he came to Bombay and settled there along with a new chamber and a house. In Bombay he got some confidence about his profession. But time never allowed him to stand on his own plans. This was proved when again Gandhi received a cable from South Africa to return as soon as possible. Reminding his promise with South African Community, Gandhi returned to South Africa in the year 1902. This time he went with a heavy heart without his family. Going from certain to uncertain life was painful for him because he went breaking up of a settled establishment.

Here in South Africa a variety of incidents conspired and brought him in close contact with people of many creeds and communities. He practised in Durban as a barrister. He with help of Sjt. Madanjit started a journal named *Indian Opinion*, in 1904 with its first editor Sjt. Mansukhlal. But Gandhi was practically incharge of the journal because Mansukhlal never ventured to write on intricate South African problems. Gandhi poured out his soul in its columns and expounded the principles and practices of *Satyagraha* as was understood by him those days. "Satyagraha in South Africa was not possible without Indian Opinion, said Gandhi".[12] He also worked there as a legel adviser and there he was called by a fine name 'Bhai' till he remained in South Africa. The black plague which broke in South Africa and his efforts for rescue and help made him much popular and enhanced his influence. Later Gandhi went and settled in Johanesburg. Here he got new experiences and food for his thought from Zulu rebellion. This war, said Gandhi, was not a war but a man's hunt. This gave a deep shock in the mind of Gandhi and took vow to observe *Brahmacharya* for the whole life because life without this appeared to him as animal like. *Brahmacharya*, which was observed by Gandhi willy-nilly since 1900 was sealed with a vow in the middle of 1906. At this time Gandhi, under influence of events, tried to coin a new word for Indians Movement to designate their struggle. He offered a prize through Indian Opinion to the readers to make suggestions for the same. Maganlal Gandhi coined the word *Sadagraha*, which was changed by Gändhi to Satyagraha. He for the first time experienced a jail life in 1908 for two months in South Africa for organising peaceful and non-violent movement in Transval against the Registration Act. After sometime he was jailed for second time in Pretoria.

During his jail life Gandhi was not allowed to add salt to the food during or after cooking. Such several occasions compelled and gave such an impact that Gandhi continued his food without salt for an unbroken ten years. He also experimented a saltless and pulseless diet on many of his co-workers in South Africa. In the year 1912 he visited Tolstoy's farm along with Mr. Kallenbach. He started fasting on the experiment of fruit diet at the farm. He was such a person who observed this fasting with the Hindu month of *Shravan* and the Islamic month of *Ramzan.* Here Gandhi found and revealed the secret of fasting, that fasting is the means to the end of self restraint. Becoming father of the farm Gandhi decided to find out by experience and experiment, the true system of education for the training of the young. In the farm Gandhi led his life as a school master and imparted vocational training, literary training and character building.

Gandhi launched his final struggle in South Africa in the year 1913 against the marriage recognition of the South African. The cape Supreme Court in 1913 in its judgement had held that all marriages except performed by christian rites and registered by the Registrar had no legal validity in South Africa. Against this civil discrimination under the Gandhi's leadership both men and women carried the peaceful and non-violent revolt. In this case Gandhi was trailed in Dundee and was jailed for nine months. In the second trail he was sentenced for three months imprisonment. But after six months Gandhi, Kallenbach and Polok were released from jail, Gandhi made an argument with General Smuts and as a result he suspended his *satyagraha* after reaching to an agreement in 1914. This *satyagraha* or non-violent struggle which Gandhi had started in 1906 for the course of the oppressed Indians ended in 1914 with passing of the Indian relief Bill. Thus Gandhi, a simple and professional lawyer of Indians practising in South Africa came to be regarded as a *Masiha* of the South African Indians. But Gandhi could not remain confined in South Africa only. He become known all over the world as a true humanitarian and worlds greatest social and political refomer. Still he considered for his ideas of religion and society nearer to Lord Buddha and Jesus Christ.

When Gandhi was fighting for a cause in South Africa, he came in contacts with Indian National Congress leader like Gokhale, Tilak, P. Mehta, B. Tyabj, D.E. Wacha and others. In 1914 Gandhi sailed for London to meet Gokhale whom he considered his political *guru*. But due to the outbreak of First World War Gokhale stayed in Paris. Then Gandhi in England served the English army in the war. In course of this service he met Smt Sarojini Naidu. Here the winter cold was not bearable for him, so he returned India from South Africa after earning considerable public respect in January 1915 via England after 20 years and placed himself as the disposal of his own native land. His stay in South Africa and his own bitter experiences of various acts of racial discrimination changed the entire life and action. He started his moral experiences and experiments of trying to conquor evil by love and started passive resistance by putting into practice his moral and religious ideas. All the lessons he learnt in South Africa went side by side with his life of earnest and moral practice into which he was drawn by circumstances and inner leanings whole through his life.

After arrival Gandhi met Gokhale, visited Shantiniketan, Hardwar and other places. He formed a farm, an *ashram* on 25th May 1915 at Sabarmati near Ahmedabad named Satyagraha Ashram, which later on became the centre of Gandhi's Socio-Political activities, as a training centre. Besically being a Socio-Religious thinker Gandhi took Social Service as the first and formost one. The gradual but increasing success of his method installed Gandhi in the hearts of the millions of Indians as their friend, Philosopher and guide. He was fully convinced with himself that his method of non-violent *Satyagraha* which had succeeded in solving smaller problems of life, could also be effectively applied for solving such greater problems of life either Social or Political.

We find that in the very beginning Gandhi's Satyagraha proved successful in nullifying Hindu and Muslims. But his political activities started in India from Champaran. In 1916 he delivered his first public meeting in India on the opening ceremony of the Banaras Hindu University. In 1917 the Champaran Satyagraha proved the potency of his non-violent technique. During his Champaran visit and movement Gandhi met Prof. Kripalani, Babu Rajendra Prasad and Brajkishore Prasad. Here he fought against the 'Tinkathia' system to get it abolish. Here he came in close contact with Indian peasants and in meeting with these peoples he realised and understood the reality of God, *Ahimsa* and Truth. His later faith in *Ahimsa* was his this love for the people. That day in Champaran was a red letter day for the peasents and also for Gandhi.

Gandhi fought his next political battle in Ahemdabad. He went on strike for the first time along with mill workers. To raise morals of the strikers Gandhi went on fasting for three days. At last he got success by settling the problem. This success emboldened him and he plunged into public work. He wrote several articles on the theory of capital and labour in *Young India* and *Harijan*. He proved his capability in Kheda Satyagraha where he started non-violent struggle for non-payment of land revenue to solve the financial problems of the farmers. In this work he was co-operated by his followers Vallabhbhai Patel, Shankerlal Banker, Indulal Yajnik, Mahadeo Desai and Srimati Anasuya Behan. This Kheda Satyagraha of Gandhi marked the beginning of political awakeness among the peasants and the people of India after Champaran. It gave a sign of a new life style of Indians and particularly *Satyagrahis*. As a result the farmers were exempted from paying the land revenue. This was the third victory of Gandhi in India.

In the year 1919 the Rowlatt Act, which was to rob the people of their freedom was protested by Gandhi. In protest of this act he observed *hartal* with great success, which was a peaceful protest against the evil law. By the year 1920 all the leaders like Gokhale, Tilak and others were dead. With departure of these national leaders Gandhi was left alone to lead the country for *Swaraj*. He advised the country men to surrender so generously to the British Government. He started a campaign for *boycotting* the foreign cloths and it was named *Swadeshi* movement which catalysed both the communities into action. Simplicity was the main feature of *Swadeshi Movement*. Hence Gandhi started *wearing lion cloth* to identify himself with the millions of Indians. Gandhi the half naked fakir, as told by Winston Churchil, gave a new example of simplicity to the Indians. After non-cooperation Gandhi was imprisioned in March 1922 for six years and was kept in Yeravada jail. But he was released in February 1924 on medical ground. After coming from jail he devoted his time to the propogation and implementation of the constructive programme and the organisational problem of the congress. In the All India Congress session at Lahore in 1929 Gandhi took a plea of *Poorna Swaraj* he called to boycott legislature and the committees constituted by the British Government. He also launched a civil disobedience movement in the form of *Salt satyagraha* in March 1930. Gandhi led the historic march of Dandi and broke the salt law, and afterwards this movement continued the boycott of foreign clothes and British goods. Again he was put behind the bars and was soon released on January 1931. The year 1929 was infact the year of true leadership because this year he became the leader of the Indian National Congress. The year 1931 proved the landmark because in this year Gandhi signed with Irwin a pact known as Gandhi-Irwin pact. He went to London in 1931 to attend the 2nd Round Table conference, but it proved fruitless for him and he returned to India with complete dissatisfaction. As a result of the failure of London conference a great unrest broke all over the country and civil disobedience movement came again in full swing, and Gandhi was again imprisoned in Yeravada jail. In Yeravada jail he went on fast unto death against the divide and rule policy of British Government to give the status of separate electorate to the depressed classes. As a result of his fasting, the separate electorate law was withdrawned. Then Gandhi turned his attention to social services to remove all social evils. He devoted whole of his time for the upliftment of the Harijans. He strongly criticized untouchability and advocated for dountrodden masses a respective and honourable place in the society. Untouchability abolition week throughout the country was observed from September 27 to October 2, 1932. He gave them a place of honour saying that to serve them is to serve god and called them Narayan, *Hari-ka-jan*. In 1933 he went throughout the country in the service of the Harijans. In 1942 Gandhi refused to accept the Cripps Mission and started non-violent Satyagraha. In Bombay Congress the resolution of quit India was passed and in August 1942 Gandhi called the country men to get India free giving a slogan 'Do or die'. He was soon arrested and was released after a great upheavel. In the same year he lost his faithful Mahadeo Desai and his wife Kasturba in 1944. After a hot consideration and discussion with leaders of Muslim League Gandhi accepted India's partition and India became free on 15th of August 1947.

In 1947 on the eve of Independence day and partition of India there outbroke communal disturbances in several parts of the country. Gandhi worked to a great extent to maintain Hindu-Muslim unity. He was shocked so much that he did not celebrate the Independence day as he thought that independence was tainted communal disturbance. Such was the man he, a man of principles, love and emotions. B. R. Nanda rightly commented that Gandhi was deeply human and almost sentimental even in politics.[13]

After independence Gandhi decided to devote himself to the social service to the Hindu-Muslim unity and the problem of refugees. Unfortunately such a sage of non-violence and staunch believer in communal unity was assassinated by a Hindu young Indian on January 30, 1948. On this day a becon light had gone out of India's heart which was a irrepable loss for our country. The whole life of Mahatma Gandhi from 1869 to 1914 and from 1915 to 1948 became a household story not only of Indians, but of the entire world. For him the political freedom of India was only an important means for extension of his method of non-violence for the solution of other problems in India and the world at large.

As Social Thinker and Reformer of the Modern Age

Mahatma Gandhi was not a Social and Political leader in South Africa nor in India. He was infact a practical Idealist, a Socio-political reformer, India and the world had ever produced. He was an idealist on account of the fact that he believed in an ideal through and through spiritual. He was in true manner a practical philosopher because he always tried to put his ideas into practice. His theory of practicality developed some views regarding society, state and other institutions. He tried and proved in a concrete manner that his ideas are not merely fanciful flights of the speculative faculties of a thinker-they could be used and practiced. He was neither an academic Sociologist nor a systematic political philosopher. In order to know his thoughts and ideas about the society and state it is essential to go through his speeches and writings.

In Social and Political field Gandhi reflects on the problems relating to Society and State, but not with the intention of a theorist. He was not interested in going through and to draw out the basis of social organisation or in evolving a theory of the state. His ideal is a practical one that of introducing certain reforms in social and political setup. His analysis of Socio-Political problems are normative and they invariably refer to an ideal to the same ideal of Truth and Non-violence upon which the entire thought system of Gandhi is built. He always discussed and highlighted the process and the way through which such a system could become a healthier.

Gandhi visualised the prevalent caste system as the burning social problems. He advocated that caste has no religious basis because it is bounded up with religion. *Varnashrama* as commonly understood and practiced is for Gandhi a monstrous parody of the original. He regarded it as travesty and mockery of the original four fold scientific divisions. According to Gandhi social inequalities and gradations of high and low are the by product of the multiple castes, society based on wrong notions like high and low by birth.

He, therefore, included the abolition of caste system and untouchability in his constructive programme and worked heart and soul for their end. In the eyes of Gandhi untouchability is a hydra headed monster; a sin, a blot, a curse and a chronic disease for mankind which has no scriptural base. He considered untouchability to be a heinous crime against humanity. "Untouchability is not only a part and parcel of Hinduism but a plague, which it is the bounded duty of every Hindu to combat.[14] He thought that sooner the caste described as untouchability would be abolished, the better would be for Hinduism and India. The primary work adopted by him to work for its extinction. He said that the primary duty of any caste abolitionists is to help for its removal. He exhorted the caste abolitionists to hold their soul in patience and join the battle against the common and admitted evil of untouchability. The most effective way showed by Gandhi to do away with it is to take recource of suffering, sacrifices, dedication and purity of personal character of the reformers. He believed that with the throwing away of the phenomenon of casteism by the society, the sad panoramas of caste would vanish automatically and there would remain only four classes based on hereditary callings. He said that "if one take untouchability out, the fabric of caste is destroyed. One who claims superiority at one forfeits his claim to be called a man. So arrogation of a superior status by any of the varnas over another is a denial of the law."[15]

Gandhi took strong note of the evil of untouchability prevalent in the society and worked with every bit of energy to end the age long prejudices of Sanatanists against the untouchables. He launched Satyagraha again and again to save them from inhuman treatments. To remove it he considered work propoganda and lip propoganda. During his Satyagraha he underwent fast unto death and set out on tours several times to remove their sufferings. He included entrance of untouchables in Hindu temples because it was message of freedom to the untouchables. This work was done by Gandhi with full vigour during the years 1932 and 1933 in places like Travancore, Guruvayur, Rohed, Dharwad and Belgaum. He also delivered speeches at several places and published his views in the weekly paper *Harijan* in 1932. He undertook Satyagraha to open temples, roads, wells, schools, tanks etc. for the Harijans. The most important work in this regard was done by him in the year 1932 when he fought tooth and nail against the Mac Donald's decision of granting communal award. His Satyagraha for the abolition of casteism and untouchability awakened the Indian people from dogmatic slumber and made the Savarnas embrace the Avarnas. It paved the way for the enactment of laws against untouchability and caste system in free India. As a result of his Satyagraha the attention of the mass could be focused on the fruitlessness of the prevalent caste distinctions leading to the heinous practice of untouchability.

Gandhi was staunch believer of secularism and conceived his non-violent society on the equality of all religions saying that, "religions are different roads converging to the same point. What does it matter that we take different roads so long as we reach the same goal. There are many religions as there are individuals."[16] The true knowledge of religion breaks down the barriers between faith and faith.[17]

Gandhi advocated that a non-violent secular society will give birth to a non-violent secular state. He wrote "If I were a dictator, religion and state would be separate. I swear by my religion. I will die for it but it is my personal affair. The state has nothing to do with it. That is everybody's personal concern.[18] To attain his aim of secularism Gandhi took recourse of different techniques of Satyagraha in the year 1946, 1947, and 1948 at different places like Noakhali, Bombay, Patna, -utta and Delhi. He visited the riot affected areas and preached the internal unity of all religions and the oneness of all lives.

As Political Thinker and Reformer of the Modern Age

Apart from society, Gandhi was also convious for state because society and state are interdependent upon each other. To attain the non-violent goal he went deep through the state and politics giving new ideals to create a step in coherence with his society full of humanity and non-violence. We find two distinct political philosophies in thoughts of Gandhi. One he talks of Ramrajya, Classless and stateless society and secondly, non-violent state. Ramrajya was for him the ultimate political ideal and the creation of a non-violent state, a second best ideal.

The state according to Gandhi is compulsive which is the very antithesis on voluntariness. Real morality can be found when acts are done by the free will of the doer. No action which is not voluntary can be called moral. He said that a state of things destroys individual growth and moral freedom which are the basis of genuine progress. To Gandhi, the end is the greatest good of all and this can be realised only in the classless and stateless democracy of autonomous village communities based on non-violence.[19] Society is infact a patron and Government a publisher, because Gandhi was in favour of society. He called the people of the country to remove the inequalities because there can be no Ramrajya in the state of inequitous inequalities in which a few roll in riches and masses do not get even enough to eat.[20] He made efforts for a society in which there would be spiritual, economic and political freedom. He thought human beings to gain spiritual freedom, freedom from the slavery of animal passions, economic freedom meant freedom from exploitation and political freedom meant freedom from foreign bondage. He stressed for spiritual freedom and believed that it would ensure other kinds of freedom which would be permanent and lasting. His concept of state always stood for a non-violent and democratic order with moral values forming the base of non-violent democratic order. His theory of Ramrajya amounted to the synthesis of the Augustinian conception of the kingdom of god on earth with the democratic ideal of the sovereignty of the people. It can be also regarded as a realisation of the synthesis of the Thomistic conception of natural law and the Rousseanic conception of general will.

Thus the aim of *Satyagraha* of Gandhi was not merely transfer of power from white man to the brown men but also at setting up a democratic form of Socio-political order. He said that in absence of new order, freedom is a cry in the wildnerness. In course of his Satyagraha struggles in India, his immediate objective in the political sphere was the highest form of political order that men had till then envisaged. A non-violent political order in the eyes of Gandhi gurantees national existence on the basis of co-operation, harmony and individual freedom. He pleaded for a democratic form of socio-political order, but he was against its western form because western democracies were democracies in name only as they practised violence and gave little place to individual freedom. In *Hind Swaraj* he had vehemently criticised the western democracies and gave idea of an ideal democracy. He was strong preacher of *Swaraj* and that is why he said that the European pople have political power but no Swaraj. Western parliaments were described by him as a 'Staerile Women' and 'talking shop.' He said, "what is done today may be undone tomorrow. It is not possible to recall a single instance in which finality can be predicted for its work.[21]

Mahatma Gandhi had therefore a different conception of democracy, a democracy being product of truth and non-violence. True democracy could not be worked by twenty men sitting at the centre. It had to be worked from below by the people of every village. He advocated that every village should be a republic having full power. He said that a society which provides individual freedom and practises non-violence is the basis of real democracy. In a democracy of his vision there is no place for social religious and economic inequalities. Swaraj of Gandhi's dream never reconises any race or religions distinction.

With the democratic base of society, Gandhi envisaged a democratic state and Government. He strongly advocated a state and its governments a non-violent one through and through. Realizing that a complete non-violent state is difficult, he wanted a state to become predominantly non-violent or democratic in faith and practice. In his democratic set-up Gandhi favoured indirect election because contrary to it cannot produce a sound and healthy democracy. Government in this society will be based on non-violence and persuasion will characterize its working. There will be no prison in the predominently non-violent state. He advocate to make jail a reformatory, a hospital and a school into one. He emphasises the moral or spiritual basis of society which makes his position akin that of the idealists like Green, Hegal and Kant. Like Green Gandhi maintains that the human spirit postulates freedom. But whereas for Green freedom postulates rights and rights demand the state. Gandhi belives that true freedom which means self-discipline and self-control or inner Swaraj can be realized only in a condition of enlightened anarchy. Thus in the nature of the state Gandhi standed opposed to the idealist but he was very near to Marx. He was different from Marx because he emphasizes the materialistic aspect of it. Unlike Plato, Gandhi did not systematically developed his ideas of his new social order, yet its chief features can be gleaned from various utterances, beliefs and writings of.

Writer Par Excelence

Apart from being a reformer and thinker, Gandhi was a writer of the tall repute. He was not an ivory tower leader or philosopher and thinker. He had seen life and its essential aspects from very close quarters. His heart bled when he found around himself colour prejudice, caste system, untouchability etc.

He sought to establish a bond of intimacy with the people of the country with help of his writings. In his writings he emphasized the essential unity of human being and called for emotional integration among the people of India and the world. His writings were the part and parcel of his participation in social and political affairs. Along with a saint, a reformer and an idealist the most dynamic aspect of his life was his day to day life with pen and papers. As a writer, the periods of his writings can be divided into two phase. First phase, the writings during his stay in South Africa and second phase, the writings in the course of National Movement uptill his death.

In South Africa the basic feature of Natal Indian congress was propaganda. During his struggle in South Africa Gandhi wrote two pamphletes—*An Appeal to Every Indian in South Africa* and The Indian Franchise—An Appeal. It was the first occasion in the life of Gandhi to write with his own pen his views for the masses. The first pamphlet contained a statement supported by evidence of Natal Indians and the later dealt with a brief history of the Indian franchise in Natal with facts and figures. In the sake of South African Indians the Journal *Indian Opinion* was started which was edited by Gandhi. In this Journal he reflected the changes in the life and philosophy of his great experiments with truth. He expounded the principle and practice of Satyagraha. He wrote a book *Hind Swaraj* in which he depicted the importance of Satyagraha. He also translated Ruskin's *Unto This Last* into Gujarati language and entitled it Sarvodaya. This book stressed that the good of an individual is contained in the good of all. It also dealt with dignity of labour as well as the importance of man power and handicrafts.

Gandhi also edited the famous papers and Journals like *Young India, Harijan* and *Navjivan.* In *Young India* there were many articles of Gandhi on the relation between the capital and the labour; on the unity of Hindu-Muslim and other problems of India. He wrote *The Story of My Experiments with Truth,* through his journal. This continued published article in various issues of this journal had been later compiled in the form of a voluminious book by Navjivan Publishing House, Ahmedabad in 1927.

The first issue of *Harijan Weekly* was published by and for the servants of untouchables society from Poona on the 11th of February 1933. Gandhi used the column's of this weekly to explain the various national issues including castes system and untouchability. His writings in this weekly enlightened the people social fields, *Swadeshi,* co-operation, non-violence and the relation between labour and capital. He also explained the role and life style of the ideal legislators through this weekly.

The monthly journal *Navjivan* in Gujarati was published and managed by Indulal Yajnik, Shankerlal Banker and Umar Sobhani. They placed this journal at the disposal of Gandhi. Gandhi later edited and controlled it into a weekly. *Young India* was at first published by these people as a weekly magazine, but Gandhi made it biweekly. *Navjivan* also dealt with Satyagraha, constructive work and other current social, political and economic problems of the country.

He also wrote many books and I have mentioned very few of them. His other important books are *Satyagraha in South Africa, Delhi Diary, Ethical Religion* etc. and other books written by him. His speeches and writings published in *Harijan* had been compiled in a book entitled *Speeches and Writings of Gandhi.* Thus, Gandhi was not only a Socio-Political worker, leader, idealist and reformer but was also a great thinker, writer and journalist of the modern age.

Influence upon Gandhi

The thoughts of Gandhi has an originality and freshness, but it carries on it the stamp of several influences. His character was built by the thoughts imprinted upon his mind through the imitation of parents in childhood and through some personalities and books during the school and the college days. The earliest influence that proved backbone to thoughts of Gandhi was Hindu religion and tradition. He had grown up in a family and tradition that had always respected Hinduism and

Hindu way of living, religion and worship. A religious atmosphere always surrounded him because his parents were Vaishnavata. At the stage of early childhood he went through the *Ramayana*, the *Bhagwata* and the *Manusmriti*. Going through these texts he got some glimpses of Hindu religion. These sharped his sense of morality and kindled his religious thought and insight. In his early life Gandhi also came in contact with Shravan's *Pitribhakti* and Harischandra's story during his school age. The both classical and religious drama gave a great impression of truth and devotion on the tender mind of Gandhi. These two personalities of truth a devotion became ideal of Gandhi which reminded with him from childhood uptill death.

Apart from Hinduism, Gandhi also took lessons from Jainism and Buddhism. Jainism was and still is an under current of Gujarati culture. Despite being a Vaishnava his parents regarded Jainism too. Becharji Swami, a jain monk frequently visited his home, by whom he was much impressed. Buddhism became the heart and soul of Gandhi's thought and practice. Going through the book *The Light of Asia* by Arnold, M. he came nearer to Buddha. He basically adopted the positive doctrine of non-violence from Buddhism.

Gandhi was also greatly influenced by Christianity and Islam. He studied about Christianity and was much impressed by the New Testament, specially *The Serman on the Mount*. He was influenced by the life and personality of christ, that he incorporated in his thought the original saying of christ. Gandhi was indebted for it to Tolstoy, who in his book *The Kingdom of God is Within You*, gave a new interpretation to Christianity. Tolstoy left his mark on the mind of Gandhi to such a great extent that his emphasis upon the power and dignity of suffering gave to Gandhi a great inspiration for developing his own notion of *Satyagraha*. Tolstoy's spiritual interpretation of Christianity, the presence of God in individual and his emphasis upon the Sermon on the Mount and conquering of hatred by love and evil, by non-resistence seemed to Gandhi to be in exact confirmity with Buddhist and Jains teachings about *Ahimsa* and to put into social practice. Apart from Christianity, Gandhi was influenced by Islam to a far extent. He went through the sale's translation of *Quran* and came to know that Islam is not a religion of coercion and violence but one of the inspired religion. He wrote in *Harijan* in 1940 that the superiority of non-violence over violence has always been shown in the *Quran*, which shows that how much he was impressed by the Islamic religion.

In England he also learnt about greatness, bravery and austere, living of prophet from Carlyle's Heroes and Hero worship. from his legal studies he learnt two great things, firstly, the maxims what the two third of law are facts and secondly, the idea of trusteeship. He also came in contact with two Theosophists who told him about the *Geeta.* He also studied Sir Edwin Arnold's english translation of *Geeta.* The idea of duty contained in the Geeta has greatly shared in the formation of the Gandhian idea of Satyagraha. The last 19 verses of the second chapter contain for me all knowledge and are the key to the interpretation of the Geeta clearly defines how balanced state of mind can be achieved.[22]

Raichand Bhai, a man of towering influence, a Saintly Indian in South Africa a man of ideal Hindu life, made a deep impression upon Gandhi. I must say that no one else except Raichand Bhai has ever made on me the impression that Raichand Bhai did. His words went straight home to me.[23] Apart from Raichand Bhai, Gandhi was influenced by the ideal personality of Chaitanya Deo, Narshim Mehta, Sita, Prahlad, Meerabai and Ashoka to such a deep sense that he called them true *Satyagrahi.*

Ruskin's *Unto This Last* has also been one of the transforming influence that shaped the views, thoughts and experiments of Gandhi. He was also specially influenced by Ruskin's ideal of manual labour. Unto this last brought an instaneous and practical transformation in Gandhi and he arose with the down. This book had such a great impact that he translated the book into Gujrati and named it *Sarvodaya.* From this book Gandhi drew the idea of the Sarvodaya, the good of individual is contained in the good of all.

Thoreau made no less influence upon Gandhi is strengthning, widening and confirming his idea of *Satyagraha.* Thoreau impressed him greatly through his essay civil Disobedience and this eassy made him a stanuch preacher of civil disobediece and non-cooperation. Gandhi adopted the principles of Thoreau down to his heart, thoughts and deeds. This civil disobedience of Thoreau became not only a technique but part and parcel of Gandhian Satyagraha.

Thus what Gandhi appeared before us is nothing but a platform of scholarly thoughts and actions assembled. What he did in his life is an outcome of his prophetic character made by the above said sources of influences-religions, books and personalities. Gandhi himself claimed that three moderns have left a deep impression on my life and he was captivated by Raichand Bhai by his living contact, Tolstoy by his book *The Kingdom of God is within You,* and Ruskin by his *Unto This Last.*[24]

While Gandhi occupied in waging liberation struggle first is south Africa and then in India by his writings and practice, at the same time he was evolving a philosophy or a way of life which can be called revolutionary. Inspite of deeply influenced by ancient Indian tradition, Gandhi was radical and revolutionary. Pleading for a stateless society he proved himself more revolutionary than Marx and Kropotkin. He denounced the utilitarian principle of the greatest good of the greatest number and gave the theory of Sarvodaya. He presented a revolutionary doctrine of spiritual common wealth more revolutionary than that of stocics and the Christian thinkers. He gave a great challenge to the fundamental basis of Western Civilization and culture which none of the modern thinkers ever did - 'the supermacy of matter over spirit'. He emphasised on the spiritual aspect of life and his conviction that matarialism finally yield place to spiritualism in which alone lies the hope of the individual and mankind from various fetters.

Going through the life, practices and experiments of Gandhi we can arrive at a point that the Gandhian thought is through and through spiritualistic in nature. Writings, meditations and actions of the affairs of life runs a silken thread of his faith in truth, love and non-violence, but the spiritual side is the permanent side of human nature. The faith of Gandhi in God is as much hard as the granite rocks. Spiritualism is thus the sheet anchor and the nerve centre of Gandhi's thought. All his ideas such as materialistic affairs of life, the economic organisation of the society, trusteeship, science and technology came out and gained stability from his spiritual convictions. He advocated a life in complete harmony between physical and psychological needs to attain the complete development of spiritual part.

Gandhi was unique among all great one's of all times because he was the man who gave idea of *Swaraj* in individual and general, social and political and tried to evolve a philosophy of life which has its paramount validity. He dacked his stages of life with marvellous thoughts and deeds which influenced the thinking, feeling and actions of people through generations and revolutionized the whole world of thought and ideas. The way he ruled the hearts and mind of the people and gave *Satyagraha* made such a light that the whole of the galaxy of the greats dimmed in the dazzling light embodied by him. He made himself great through struggles and experiments with help of two qualities-Love for truth and Love of all fellow beings. His life denotes that even an ordinary man and women has within his/her a capacity to attain perfection which can create miracle. Tagore described him as "the great soul in a begger's grab" and called him "Mahatma", who became the model of humility. Out of his whole life story which he called `a series of experiments with truth' one can know and understand the whole of the edifice of his philosophy-thoughts and Experiments. He was a strange alchemy about whom we of this generation can scarcely believe that a man such as him ever walked the face of this earth. He not only walked but carried thousands and millions of people with him in the struggle for freedom like none has wirnessed or is likely to witness in the future.

But besides his such a greatness there remained something wrong in Gandhi which if considered to a far extent would draw or reveal the actual state where Gandhi was his personality, essence and status. Simply Gandhi was a humble and sincere follower of Sanatana Dharma, a *Vanaprastha*, a man striving for *moksha*. He simply renovated the age old philosophy. He was infact a good interpreter and a skilled decorator, by interpreting age old thought from past to present decorating by new terms. In reality he was not the father of any of his own thought but was a mere follower and great teacher who taught to mankind the thoughts of great one's and proved their applicability and relevancy to the modern context. Therefore, no doubt Gandhi was great for his art of teaching but he was not the propounder. He simply adopted in its totality worlds existing religions, personalities like Christ, Tolstoy, Ruskin, Thoreau and going through the story of his whole life we always find Gandhi simply as a man advocating what has been told before him. But all these should be taken into account in an another chapter entitled criticism and negative impact.

REFERENCES

1. M. K. Gandhi, *The story of My Experiments with Truth*, p. 10.
2. M. K. Gandhi, *Autobiography*, by Mahadeo Desai, p. 17.
3. M. K. Gandhi, *Autobiography*, by Mahadeo Desai, p. 17.
4. M. K. Gandhi, *Autobiography*, by Mahadeo Desai, p. 17.
5. M. K. Gandhi, *My Experience with Truth*, by Mahadeo Desai, p-41.
6. M. K. Gandhi, *Me Experience with Truth*, by Mahadeo Desai, p. 41.
7. M. K. Gandhi, *Autobiography*, by Mahadeo Desai, p. 51.
8. M. K. Gandhi, *Autobiography*, by Mahadeo Desai, p. 67.
9. M. K. Gandhi, *Autobiography*, by Mahadeo Desai, p. 69.
10. M. K. Gandhi, *Autobiography*, by Mahadeo Desai, p. 129.
11. M. K. Gandhi, *Autobiography*, by Mahadeo Desai, p. 159.
12. M. K. Gandhi, *Autobiography*, by Mahadeo Desai, p. 211.
13. Nanda, B.R., *Biography*, p. 120

14. M. K. Gandhi, *From Yeravada Mandir*, p. 31.
15. M. K. Gandhi, *The Removal of Untouchability*, p. 36.
16. M. K. Gandhi, *Hind Swaraj* or *Indian Home Rule*, p. 23.
17. M. K. Gandhi, *Yeravada Mandir*, p. 40.
18. M. K. Gandhi, *In Search of the Supreme*, Vol. II, p.329.
19. Dhawan, G. N., *The Political Philosophy of Mahatma Gandhi*, p.5.
20. M. K. Gandhi, *Non-Violence in Peace and War* Vol. II, p.248.
21. M. K. Gandhi, *Hind Swaraj*, p. 16.
22. M. K. Gandhi, *Young India . II*, p. 935.
23. M. K. Gandhi, *Autobiography*, by Desai M., Navjivan Press.
24. M. K. Gandhi, *Autobiography*, by Desai, Navjivan Press, p. 65.

1

MEANING AND OBJECTIVE OF SATYAGRAHA

In the previous chapter we went through the brief life sketch of the Mahatma and found several theories in practice. But it is noteworthy here that all his thoughts and experiments are based on *Satyagraha*—a method of political action which suited the resistance of a disarmed people against a mighty power. Through his teachings and experiments Gandhi demonstrated to the world that Satyagraha is a successful alternative to violence with all its Hindu Orientation, a strong revolutionary action from the proletarian revolutionary action in its advocacy of Non-violence. Beside Gandhi, Vinoba can claim to have been so close to Gandhi spiritually and conscious, intelligent and objective , an observer and student of Gandhi since 1916 upto his last moment. No one except Vinoba dedicated himself to Gandhian thought. But he never surrender his judgements blindly to his Guru. He was not a stickler with words of Gandhi. He never repeated Gandhi and after Gandhi he thought furiously how to apply Gandhian thought. He explained the doctrine of Gandhian thought and said about Gandhi and his principles, his own ideas and thoughts which went something different from Gandhi in the context of the age, the age of Gandhi and post Gandhian age. Where there is some talks about Gandhi, it is necessary to talk about Vinoba that what at early stage in life let him to seek the Mahatma and as to how right from the start Gandhi as possessed and in due course saturated him.[1] Here in this chapter we will discuss upon the Satyagraha of Gandhi and post Gandhian Satyagraha advocated by Vinoba.

Satyagraha, a term evolved for the first time by Mahatma Gandhi in South Africa to give distinctive identity to his Non-violent movement against racial discrimination was coined by Gandhi himself from two

Sanskrit words *Satya (Truth)* and *Agraha (Insistence or determined pursuit or holding on to truth).* Truth infact is a transcendental value encompassing all existence of life and time. The pursuit of truth must be through Non-violence. For Gandhi Truth and Non-violence are identical terms and these both together constitute the sum and substance of Satyagraha.

To a man in the street or to an unsophisticated villager, Satyagrha is stood for Gandhi's way of fighting, a technique for solving conflict and a method for fighting against evil. Gandhi was aware that a theoretical emphasis on the value and importance of Truth and Non-violence would lead unless a way is shown for the practice of Non-violence that took him to develop a technique to Non-violence to which he named *Satyagraha,* which he called love force, soul force and truth force. Gandhi went on throughout his life making newer and newer experiments with his new techniques and thus succeeded in giving to it a definite shape. Satyagraha thus is a vindication of truth not by infliction of suffering on the oponent but one's own self.

Gandhi derived his idea of Satyagraha neither from Christ nor from Tolstoy, but from his own Vaishnavite faith. The technique or as Gandhi puts, 'the Science of Satyagraha' was discovered by him which he himself called a series of experiments with truth. One can know and understand the whole of edifice of his philosophy of Satyagraha in the course of his Non-violent movements.

Earlier Gandhi described his movement (technique) as passive resistance, a nomenclature borrowed from Christian and Pacifist literature and practices in the West. But Gandhi was not satisfied with the expression 'passive' and he was at pains to distinguish between Passive resistance and Non-violent resistance. As his movement advanced Gandhi was in search for a suitable expression in place of passive. Maganlal Gandhi suggested the term *Sadagraha*, a combination of to Sanskrit words *Sat* and *Agraha* (Truth and Firmness) which after a slight modification by the Mahatma became Satyagraha, a composition of Satya and Agraha containing a literal meaning, holding on to truth or firmness on truth. It is an expression of looking at a life and away of living. His philosophy of life and method of opposing of evil are both called *Satyagraha*. It is on the one hand eminently more than and anarchial moral principle and on the other hand it does not make requisite those aspects of Gandhian technique which specify rules of individual self-leaving because Satyagraha is basically and ethnic principle, the essence of which is a social technique of action.

Gandhi use the term passive resistance in course of his struggle, his Non-violent movement against racial discrimination which was later named *Satyagraha.* He use passive resistance in the sense of Satyagraha. Passive resistance described by Gandhi in the *Hind Swaraj*, in the seventeenth chapter entitled 'Passive Resistance', is a real discription of Satyagraha. He was concious that passive resistance was a popular but less adequate and accurate description of Satyagraha then soul force or love force.[2] This change was necessary because passive resistance was found by Gandhi that it is too narrowly constructed as a weapon of weak and it admitted the inner hatret that could finally lead to violence.

Satyagraha on the other hand was adopted because it is one of the strong firmness and determination without any scope for the use of arms. Physical force is forbidden even in the most favourable circumstances. In it the use of violence in any form is totally rulled out even against manifestly weaker one's. The aim of passive resistance is to embrass and harass the adversery and eventually to defeat. But in Satyagraha the accent is on not causing the slightest harassment or injury to the opponents. Satyagraha is applicable to all contexts and situations, equal or unequal, and is based on fundamental philosophical, ethical, psychological assumptions rationally and empirically perceived, Satyagraha is thus like passive resistance, a holistic doctrine or a way of life aiming at the creation or restoration of normal life through normal means. Passive Resistance thus used in the orthodox English sense and covers the suffragette movement as well as the resistance of the Non-Conformists. Satyagraha, then is literally holding on to truth. It is active Non-violence, all pervasive creed and technique. Non-violence to be a creed has to be all pervasive. One cannot be Non-violent about one's activity of himself and violent about others. If one does not practice Non-violence in one's personal relations with others and hopes to use it in bigger affairs, one is vastly mistaken. Non-violence like charity must begin at home. One cannot be Non-violent in one's own circle and violent outside it. The law must apply to nations as to individuals. Thus Satyagraha covers family relations, relations with constituted authority, internal disorders and external aggression, put in another way it covers all human relations.

Thus alphabet of Satyagraha is best learnt in the domestic school and if one gets secure success here, one and all are sure to do so everywhere else. For a *Satyagrahi* the whole world is one family. It may be undertaken by a son against his father and father against his son; by the pupils in a school against the headmaster or by the latter against the former. It can be taken by one set of relations against another even among near and dear one's, and in the most intimate relations like between a husband and wife. Gandhi described such one under the caption 'Domestic Satyagraha'. He insisted that Satyagraha is only an extension of domestic Satyagraha and that every case of the former should be tested by imagining a parallel domestic case.[3] Satyagraha must be placed before everything else while it is professed. Then alone it becomes irresistable. Otherwise it will be only an empty bulk, a thing without potency or power.[4]

Satyagraha is essentially based upon love. It appears to Gandhi as a religious pursuit and rests on a religious belief that there is one God, who resides in everyone. This is the basis of love, and unless one has this basis of love for mankind, one cannot practice the doctrine of Satyagraha. Belief in rebirth is also a precondition of Satyagraha. It demands a selfless and sincere pursuit of truth without any consideration of any advantage or gain. The spiritual and moral weapon in Satyagraha, as conceived by Gandhi in South Africa was employed in a more comprehensive and wider sense. Gandhi himself said that I am myself daily growing in the knowledge of Satyagraha. Satyagraha as conceived by me is science in the making.[5] The science of Satyagraha came to Gandhi by scientific approach and research. It was a result of the hardest labour a human being is capable of. I have applied to this research all the skill of scientist.[6] Satyagraha is nothing but the implementation of truth and Non-violence in different walks of life. Truth and Non-violence are virtues not only of individuals, but of the whole humanity. Gandhi said, I mean to suggest that truth and Non-violence were not virtues confined to individuals but were practised by communities. To me virtue ceases to have any value if it is cloistered or possible only for individuals.[7]

Gandhi wielded the moral weapon of Satyagraha to end domestic, social, political, economic, religious and cultural problems and conflicts. His autobiography is full of his own Satyagraha in his family life. Experimenting it in his own domestic sphere, Gandhi observed that Non-violence or Satyagraha in politics is a new weapon in process of evolution.[8] Non-violence for him is the universal law acting under all circumstances not merely to settle family disputes, but also to solve group conflicts. In fact it is the moral equivalent to war. It can be used by individuals in their daily life in relation to parents, children, friends and even criminals and sub-human relations and creations. In words of Gandhi, it is a force that may be used as will in political as in domestic affairs. In universal applicability is a demonstration of its permanence and incivility.[9] For Gandhi the law of Satyagraha is an eternal principle. I co-operate with all that is good and desired to non-cooperate with all that is evil, Whether it is associated with my life, son or myself.[10] Thus Gandhi nursed Satyagraha up into the mighty weapon capable of being wielded by large masses of men and women, for his long experienced right from childhood and onwards in the working of the law of love in his personal life.

Non-violent Satyagraha begins and ends by turning the inward searchlight. The employment of Satyagraha against others must be preceeded by its application against one's own self, the intelligent cultivation of Non-violent values. The self discipline which includes control of thought and emotions, life and commitant ethical beliefs. While on the other hand passive resistance is a mare technique of fighting wrongs or a policy followed by the unarmed against superior force apparantly an expedient device. The difference between the two is due to the fact that passive resistance is a political weapon of expediency but Satyagraha is a moral weapon based upon the superiority of soul force over physical force.

Passive Resistance is practised from an awareness of weakness or helplessness, vis-a-vis the strong adversery. Gandhi himself observed passive resistance as a weapon of the weak.[11] Satyagraha on the other hand is practised from a sense of strength arising from a belief in the essential goodness of human nature and its responsiveness to voluntary self-suffering and sacrifice. Satyagraha believing a satyagrahi to be strong, two consequences comes from it. Firstly fostering the idea of strength one grow stronger and stronger every day and a result of it Satyagraha too becomes more effective.

In passive resistance there is a reason for the violent methods or practices as sabotage or secracy in a suitable opportunity. While in Satyagraha one is to stick to what is true and right at all costs and secrifices. Gandhi took it as the means of realization of truth and also carried for him the implication of the method of love. Gandhi himself said that the term passive resistance is an insufficient expression. He rejected passive resistance because of its insufficiency and its being interpreted as a weapon of the week.[12]

Satyagraha and passive resistance are methods of mesting aggression, setting conflicts and bringing about social and political changes. But the two differs fundamentally. Former differs from latter as the North Pole differs from South. Gandhi himself noted the difference saying that there is a great and fundamental difference between the two. If without understanding this , those who call themselves either passive resister or Satyagrahi believe both to be one and same, there would be injustice to both leading to untoward consequences.[13] Satyagraha is essentially different from what we generally mean in English by the phrase 'Passive Resistance'.[14]

Satyagraha as conceived and practised by Gandhi is a matter of faith or creed grounded in an integrated philosophy of the universe, develops in the *Satyagrahi* the inner strength, the soul force that becomes irresistable. Satyagrahi is essentially a man of peace and that is the beauty of Satyagraha. It comes up to one's self, one has not to go in search for it, and this is a virtue inherent in the principle itself. A struggle previously planned is not a righteous struggle.

Satyagraha can be undertaken for social good and not for personal gain; for one who cannot rise above the personal interest is unfit to be true Satyagrahi.[15] It is infact not a light hearted affair. Its moral requirements are exacting. A Satyagrahi observes perfect chastity, adopt poverty, follow truth and cultivate fearlessness. A Satyagrahi bids goodbye to fear. Even if the opponent plays him false twenty time, a Satyagrahi is ready to trust him twenty first time, for an implicit trust in human nature is the very essence of his creed.[16] The soul of Satyagraha is the active resistance that finds its outlet in the sacrifice of one self which is suffering, because suffering is the law of life. For example, the mother suffers so that the child may live and the seed perishes so that the seedling may grow. One must not forget the distiction between the evil and the evil doer, for love is the motive force of Satyagraha. The only way to purge the world of evil by trying to overcome evil by good, anger by love, untruth by truth and *himsa* by *ahimsa*, and all these are found are in Satyagraha. Gandhi strongly condemned violence and other's saying that the greater will be the violence, the weaker will be the revolution. So he adopted this unique technique Satyagraha. It is in fact the relentless pursuit of truthful ends by non-violent means. Gandhi emphasized upon the means and said that even the goal of a Satyagrahi is good, he should be scruplous about his employed means. He strongly rejected the Machiavellian argument that the end justifies the means. He considered it to be a grevious error to hold that there is no connection between the means and the ends. One cannot grow a rose through planting a noxious weed. The means may be linked to a seed and end to a tree. Opposed to end justifies the means, Gandhi advocated, means justifies the end. He points out that if I want to deprive you of your watch, I shall have to fight for it; and if I want to buy your watch, I shall have to pay for it; and if I want it as a gift, I shall have to plead for it; and according to the means I employ the watch is stolen property, my own property or a donation. Thus motive determines the means and it in turn effects the end. Purity of motive leads to purity of means and it in turn produces good end Non-violence or Satyagraha is thus the means to attain good end. Satyagraha is the way of non-violence, and therefore justified that it is the right course at all time and all places. The power of arms is violence and condemned as such in all religions. Infact there are no limits on Satyagraha and non except those placed by the Satyagrahi's capacity for tapascharya, for voluntary suffering. It if started is not decided by any mathematical rule.

In Satyagraha, there is no room for hatred, where self reliance is the order of the day, where no one looks at another, where are no leaders and no followers, and so the death of a fighter makes not for slackness but on the other hand intensifies the struggle. Such is the pure and essential nature of Satyagraha, said Gandhi.[17] The very nature of Satyagraha is such that the fruit of the movement remains contained in the movement itself. It is based on self-help, self-sacrifice and faith in God.

The meaning of Satyagraha itself reveals that the first condition to become a Satyagrahi is to show a special regard for truth and have the strength that flows from truthfulness. Such a man should depend on truth. One cannot have the best of both the two worlds. A man who attempts to have it is crushed under preassure of both kinds, of physical strength and moral argument. This reveals the fact that one cannot have one foot in curds and the other in milk. Satyagraha is thus not a carrot to be played on as a pipe. Here it becomes clear that it should be wrong to assess that Satyagraha is being restored to only by those who are deficient in physical strength or who finding physical strength unavailing can think of nothing but Satyagraha. Those who hold such a view do not know what this fight means.

Satyagraha is more potent then physical strength, which is worthless as straw when compared with the former. Physical strength means that a man of such strength fights on the battle field with little regard for his body. A Satyagrahi on his part, gives no thought to his body and fear does not tuch him at all. That is why he does not arm himself with any material weapon and takes resistance to larger extent till the end without any fear of death. Thus the Satyagrahi possesses more courage than a man who relies on physical strength. Pursuit of truth and faith in truth is necessary for a satyagrahi. He must be indifferent to wealth, because wealth and truth have always been in conflict with each other. But this does not mean that a Satyagrahi can have no wealth. A Satyagrahi can have wealth but he cannot make his wealth his God. He cannot allow himself to be an accomplice in tyranny. in such circumtances a Satyagrahi remains content and thinks himself rich in his poverty. A Satyagrahi is also bound to break away from family attachments. This proves that the practice of Satyagraha is like walking on the edge of a sword. Also a Satyagrahi is obliged to suffer hunger and thirst to bear heat and cold, to sacrifice family bounds and to put up with pecuniary loss.

Thus we find that one can alone offer Satyagraha who has true faith in religion. Anyone who has true religion and faith in God can offer Satyagraha. He who leaves everything to God can never know defeat in this world. The real nature of Satyagraha in that one who has sacrificed everything for Satyagraha has gained everything for he lives in contentment. Satyagraha can be offered without thinking of the result. It is in fact a kind of education in the real sense of the term.[18] If we undergo education with a specific object in view such as earning our livelihood, the education will not be wasted even though we fail to earn the objective. In the same way the invaluable education of Satyagraha, the benefit received through the strengthening of will power which results from our adherence to truth and suffering is never lost. Those who become Satyagrahi and remains so, reaps the fruits of Satyagraha in any part of the Globe where ever they move.

But like everything else, Satyagraha has also its limits.[19] To understand how much one can achieve through it is in fact the very first step to success in it. For one and all the path of truth is not meant for ends, not consistant with truth. Many things can be achieved through Satyagrah, but one fails to achieve if one doesnot compromise in one's regard for truth.

Not to enhance our original demands is the first and formost principle of Satyagraha. Secondly, what is obtained by Satyagraha can be retained only by Satyagraha. Thirdly, what ever is attainable by Satyagraha cannot but be achieved and Satyagraha knows no word such as defeat. Anger and pride, ego and weakness are important limitations of Satyagraha. It would be better if instead we gave up the very name Satyagraha and behaved as we thought best.[20] One who has not had some training in constructive work has not even learnt the first steps in Satyagraha. By constructive work Gandhi means the spinning wheel and khadi work, removal of untouchability, work for prohibition, striving for friendship between the Hindus, Muslims, Sikhs and Christians. He who is not imbued with the spirit of service and the spirit of love could never dream of offering Satyagraha.[21] One who is by nature Non-violence who is by temperament Satyagrahi, in whom truth pervades and who has the spirit of service embodied deserves the respect of the world and needs neither any advice nor any guidance.

But one who is full of anger and pride, whose ego fills their being and whose intellect is disturbed by passion, Gandhi suggests such people to hold their patience. I would certainly say, please hold yourselves in patience. Any thoughtless step would lead to bitter consequences and would also destroy the little control that would produce suffering at present and future on account of the so-called Satyagraha will curse and the very name Satyagraha will suffer disrepute. Every thoughtful person should, therefore, appreciate the limitations of Satyagraha.[22] The aim of Satyagraha is to train the sufferrer by actual demonstration as to how one can free oneself from his sufferings. Thus the limitations of Satyagraha is infact its beauty and strength. The Satyagrahi does not become anyone's patron or gurdian. He suffers with the sufferer and becomes partner of suffering. The world rests upon the bedrock of Satya or Truth. Asatya or untruth also means Non-existent and Satya or Truth also means that which is. If untruth doesnot so much as exist, its victory is out of question, and truth being that which is can never be destroyed. This is the doctrine of Satyagraha in a nutshell.[23] It is infact a relentless search for truth and a determination to reach truth.[24] One of the axioms of religion is that there is no religion other than truth. So it follows that truth is love and love is truth. Truth force than is love force. In thousands of our acts the propelling power is truth or love, and we apply Satyagraha consciously or unconciously in regulating all kinds of human realtions. In India we have been trained from ages past in the teaching of Satyagraha, and hence it is that we are taught to consider whole universe as one family, 'Basudeo Kutumbakam'. The fullness of national life is also impossible without Satyagraha.[25] It is thus a force that works silently and apparently slow and there is no force in this world that is so direct and so swift in working.[26] It is gentle and never wounds the direct opposite of compulsion, a complete substitute for violence.[27]

Thus Satyagraha is based on the conviction that love, Non-violence and conscious suffering are the only means to over come the evil forces because this is the Divine way; the way of Truth. In fact it is the way of God, the noblest and the best education. The greater the spirit of Satyagraha in us the better men we will become. It is a force which, if it becomes universal, world revolutionize.

Vinoba Bhave was one of the most important interpreters of

Gandhi both in thought and action. Vinoba most legitimatly and appropriately follows not Gandhi the man, but Gandhi the idea. At the time of Gandhi and after, Vinoba was the nearest and truest follower of Gandhi. Vinoba in his own words viewed and interpreted an overall picture of Mahatma's thoughts and deeds. He said that the purpose of Mahatma's life was Sadbhavana and Satyagraha, the realization of God. He said that *Sarvodaya* is an idea so comprehensive in its scope but for its full implementation one must become Satyagrahi; and must see God face to face.

Vinoba gave much importance to Satyagraha. He said that the idea is that so long as we donot find a way of ending conflicts, so long as we donot transcend war, strife and much other crude devices, the world cannot be made better. For this Satyagraha is the means.[28] Satyagraha means Non-violent insistence on truth and thus it is an application of Non-violence.

Gandhi got built the spiritual tradition of India and gave the weapon of Non-violence which was in conformity with Indian culture. Due to the spiritual tradition of India, people were so reseptive to the idea of Non-violence. The intellectual soil of India was ready for the thought of Gandhi to be planted here. The experiments of Gandhi succeeded because the essentially spiritual nature of we Indians, their compassion for all living creatures and their conviction that soul dwells in each and every living thing. That is why the whole credit for Gandhi's success does not belongs only to Gandhi himself. The credit belongs as much to the country as to Gandhi. Gandhi was only the means. If it had not been he, it would have been someone else. The power of spirit would have found one way or another to manifest itself. In fact through Gandhi India's spiritual nature came into play when the conditions were favourable for it.[29]

The uniqueness of Gandhi lay in that he was the first to apply non-violent Satyagraha on a social scale. Applying non-violence on a social scale did not occur to the people of the past ages as naturally as it was applied in the present modern age. The difference was in applied technology. Different from pre-technological age, Gandhi applied his own technology and made aware of possibility of applying soulforce on wider plane and in a gigantic scale.

Vinoba observed that the power of Satayagraha is permanent quality inherent in each and every one of us, but people fails to have correct understanding thst it is simple sticking to truth. Truth is only power which can renove the worldly violence. Truth is the supreme virtue and the *Gita* says it fearlesness. Fearlessness means fearing no one and frightening no one. To look at oneself objectively is fearlessness. *Atmanjnana* or self-knowledge is that very ablity to look at oneself in a detached way and this is the source of the power of Satyagraha. Non-violence also occupies a crucial place in Satyagraha, for in any conflict both sides fight in the name of truth.

Now a day after Gandhian Satyagraha is restored as only a matter of linguistic usage against someone. But it is not such thing as 'against'. Satyagraha is practiced 'before' someone or 'with' someone. The essence of Satyagraha is to have good intentions and to persuade the opponent to one's point and to find out one's own faults. The chief characteristic of Saytagraha is to apply thought and to develop it and understand the thought of the opponent constantly. Thought in the beginning, in the middle and in the end is the necessary law of Satyagraha. Thought in the beginning, in the end but the penance of non-violence in the middle is the contingent law of Satyagraha.[30] Satyagraha opens the doors of understanding. War stultifies thought in Satyaraha thought blossoms in the patient effort to make the other side see the truth of one's position. If the other side will be not understood in one way, one have to discover some other way, and this is the highest characteristic of Satyagraha. This is Satyagraha in its purity. It is infact not the way of coercion and this faith in the power of thought and truth is Satyagraha. The techniques of Satyagraha when where practiced by inspiration of unworthy motives is not called Satyagraha, it is called Duragraha. The power of Satyagraha does not consist in enduring suffering, but it consists in ready to suffer. Ready to suffer is one thing and using the ability to suffer as a weapon is quite another. One must be redy to put up with suffering, but in establishing truth suffering should be never taken as a condition. Thought should be the only desideratum in arriving at the truth.

Saytagraha and its underlying idea should be minutely examined and the theory must be in constant evolution. But the word 'Gandhi' serves to narrow the concept of Satyagraha. One should not think of Gandhi as a biographical character but only as an idea, and his name, therefore, ought not to be linked with Satyagraha. The character of Satyagraha can not be the same today as it was in day's of Gandhi. Times have undergone a change, which is performed and not superficial. The conditions in India and the whole have changed. Three features of the change have been especially marked by Vinoba.

1. In the day's of Gandhi we were not free.
2. In the day's of Gandhi democracy had not become established

in India.

3. The new technology was still in an incipient stage in the Gandhi's time.

Today it has developed enormously and developing day by day. These three developments after Gandhi call for a further probe into the theory of Satyagraha. He said that the theory of Satyagraha must be further developed to bring into it conformity with the changed times. It must be understood that while practice of Satyagraha with undergo changes, its essential nature, the love remains unchanged. Vinoba, a well known disciple of Gandhi, recognised that the world will not develop and trust in the power of Non-violence, untill peaceful ways have been evolved to solve the problems which the people are endeavouring to solve.[31] For this Vinoba observed that there are pre-conditions which are the secret for the success of Satyagraha.[32] He said that in modern times, after Gandhi, science has annihilated time and distance and geographically the world is now one unit. Science has brought us to the point where we may easily wipe ourselves out of existence by encouraging and aggravating the forces of violence and hatred. We can avoid it only by choosing not to tread on this path. Hatred is not likely to disappear as long as the factors which excite it are existent. A thirsty person makes search of clean water, but in absence of it, he is compelled to take unclean water. In the same way the world is not hankering after hatred. But it is faced with such problems which seeks to be solved. If they can be peacefully solved, the world has now reached the stage when it is prepared to follow the path of peace. So we Indians firstly, should strive to find out the way to produce the power of peace, to solve those problems and to establish uninterrupted peace. Thus Vinoba observed in his own words that to make Satyagraha successful one must first find out the path from which the peace comes out. The world will not developed trust in power of non-violence until this is done. It, therefore, will be a mistake to cling to those modes of Satyagraha which were current in the days of Gandhi. They were dictated by the specific condition prevailing at that time and the character of the task we pursed them was negative.[33] But the nature of the task after Gandhi is quite different. Gandhi always talked of ending or mending things, but today we cannot speak that languge. I have not slightest doubt that had Gandhi living today, he could certainly change the mode of Satyagraha. The image that we today have of Satyagraha, that were conducted during the time of Gandhi was not the image Gandhi had of them. If Gandhi were alive today he would never retain the old modes of Satyagraha.

Satyagraha today must be of a positive kind and must be very clearly defind powerful and constructive in meaning. Vinoba observed that it is wrong to think that if the pressure is greater on the opponent, Satyagraha becomes stronger in exerting that pressure. In fact, more the element of love in place of pressure Satyagraha becomes stronger. In this age of technology if Satyagraha is turned into a way of harassment, everything will become topsy-turvy and the people will lose their power of reasoning.[34]

Gandhi could not codify the theory of Satyagraha and left it to develop gradually and thus it was fallen to peoples lot to develop the modes of Satyagraha. Vinoba said that Satyagraha is a way of living, away of doing and a way of remedying, and, therofore it remains valid in all tenses past, present and future. In a democracy, there is always place for Satyagraha, though the nature of Satyagraha is sometimes found different. The word Satyagraha sounds sweet to ear and if its sound is pleasant, its results yields more satisfactory. But it would not be universal reaction to Satyagraha for mental attitudes vary from person to person. The adjective of Satyagraha should not be fiercer or fiercest, but sublime, sublimer and sublimeet. Violence is used and the desired end is not achieved, the violence is made fiarcer and when even that does not work, it is made the fiercest. But when non-violence is used and there comes no result, it is made sublimer and then sublimest. Infact the battle of non-violence is fought not outside but in one's own heart and in that of the opponent. To awaken the soul of the opponent the technique of Satyagraha is applied.

Gandhi said, resist not evil with evil. But now a day the whole context is different because the conflict is not one of passions but of ideas assailing ideas and in the process violence are used. Therefore, it is not enough to say, resist not evil but one must say, non-violent assistance in right thinking.[35] Today even violent actions call for mathematical precision and a cool mind. So when violence requires cool deliberation then there is no need of non- violence to be free from passion, and thus passion is of no use whatsover. The utmost important thing is resisting it by right thinking and Satyagraha is the only way to promote and assist right thinking. Due to these all reasons Vinoba was not happy with the term Satyagraha because he thought that the word 'agraha' is a mistake in itself. One and all should realize the truth through humility, detachment and non-insistance. Truth is not all pervasive and one and all must grab it from everywhere and that should be the main goal of a Satyagraha. Thus Vinoba said that the very first necessity of Satyagraha is that truth should itself plead for itself. Satyagraha thus is not an expedient but it is one of the eternal varieties. It should be acceptable, revered and welcome each and every moment. The attitude should be of one and all that the time of our life spent apart from Satyagraha are moments wasted.

Vinoba being the foremost disciple of Gandhi, interpreted and explained the Gandhian Satyagraha. He beautifully examined its all pros and cones in context of modern times and not fully but partly rejected its principles. He tried to find out the potency and relivency of Satyagraha in the light of modern age of science and technology. He also proposed preconditions of practising Non-violence which was a new thing in the whole idea of Satyagraha. Gandhi never talked about such conditions. Vinoba in fact developed the theory and practice of Satyagraha to make it relevent and authentic with the changing time and place. He infact changed the the language of Satyagraha spoken by Gandhi, and gave its language a new form and composition. Vinoba tried to prove the validity of Satyagraha with its changing character in every tense. He took it in its positive form and gave too much emphasis upon love. I am also fully influence of Vinoba and accept that Gandhi gave the idea of Satyagraha but it was defined and explained in its right words and path by Vinoba. In fact Satyagraha is a developing science and changes time to time and in different place. Therefore, Vinoba is a good teacher than Gandhi when he taught the whole world, the Satyagraha with Gandhi and after Gandhi, whereas Gandhi only taught Satyagraha of his own times which proved irrelevant after his days.

Objective of Satyagraha

Satyagraha can be undertaken only for social good and never for personal gain, said Gandhi.[36] This statement clearly reveals that Satyagraha is not for individual but it is for society; not for one in all but for all in one. Either individual or in a group form, Satyagraha is not in any case to crush, defeat or punish the tyrant or break his will. It is not even to harm or embrass one, though the resistance and suffering may as a fact, cause the wrong door embrassment. The essence of Non-violent technique is that it seeks to liquidate antagonisms but not the antagonish.[37] The end of Non-violent war is always an agreement, never dictation, much less humiliation of the opponent.[38]

Satyagraha thus aims at moralisation of politics, fighting injustice and tyranny, settling social, political and economic disputes, establishing effective democracy, laying the foundations of new social order based on justice and equality, paying the way for world peace. The Satyagrahi fights with a view to bilateral and not unilateral victory and aims at the integration and not suppression of legitimate differences.

The aim infact indicates the method. Gandhi worked for the conversion or correction of the wrongdoers, and Satyagraha is a process of conversion, not of coercion. Even wrongdoer would not be coerced, humiliated or harassed. Negatively the Satyagrahi tries to avoid violence in all forms. The Satyagrahi should try to avoid all intentional injury to the opponent in thoughts, words and deeds. He should not harbour anger, hatred, illwill, suspicion and other divisive feelings. As regards speech, the Satyagrahi should avoid all abusive insulting, haughty or needlessly offensive language. In his actions he should not rely on evil forces, for to do so is to co-operate with the evildoer.

A Satyagrahi will always try to overcome evil by good, anger by love, untruth by truth, and violence by Non-violence.[39] The Satyagrahi, a man conscious of the working of his soul force should treat his opponent as a member of his family. He should adopt domestic method which makes the resolution of the conflict easy by removing differences. Satyagrahi applies the same rule to the wrongdoer who is one's enemy, as well as to one's wrong doing father or son.

The idea underlying in the Satyagraha is to convert the wrongdoer, to awaken the sense of justice and to show also that without the co-operation, direct or indirect of the wronged, the wrongdoer cannot do the wrong intended by him. If the people in either case are not ready to suffer for their causes, no outside help in the shape of Satyagraha can possibly bring true deliverence.[40]

Gandhi believed that suffering is a potent and effective method of conversion, reasoning and discussion. Regarding suffering Gandhi said, if you want something really important to be done, you must not merely satisfy the reason, you must move the heart also. The appeal of the reason, is move to the head, but the penitration of the heart comes from suffering. It opens up the inner understanding in man.[41] Voluntary suffering changes the mentality of the wrongdoer and makes him to reconsider his stand, and this also arouses a sense of justice to the both. A Satyagrahi would sacrifice his own life rather than to take the opponents life. A Satyagrahi arouses a sense of justice against injustice and right against wrong in the evildoer. Even if the opponent plays false twenty times, the Satyagrahi remains ready to trust him the twenty first time, for an implicit faith in human nature is the very essence of one's creed. Gandhi was against evil, not against the evildoer. He made a clear distinction between the deed and the doer and gave emphasis upon the deed.

Mahatma Gandhi also realised that there are also such evil to which Satyagraha cannot be applied. For instance, if Government does not allow us to acquire land, Satyagraha will be of no avail. If it forbids us from walking along a certain footpath, we can resort to Satyagraha. If we are required to do anything which violates our religion or insults our method, we one and all can administer the invaluable physic of Satyagraha.[42] With the conversion of the opponent or evil doer, Satyagraha resolves conflicts of all kinds and makes it correct. As a moral weapon it is a peaceful protest against the laws, customs and practices, contrary to one's conscience, it resolves political conflicts by mutual understanding and by educating public opinion with help of reason, discussion and self-suffering. Satyagraha aims at cleansing of whole atmosphere and voluntary change of the heart and mind of all parties to a conflict. It also aims for change the inefficient, incompetent, tyrannical and unjust Governments, institutions, person or place violating the unjust and immoral political laws. As a willing obedience and voluntary co-operation, it is a substitute of forced obedience and involuntary co-operation. But it never aims at replacing democracy with anarchy. As a supplement of constitutionalism and not as its antithesis or substitute, Satyagraha has a definite place in democracy.

Gandhi preached and practised this spiritual weapon for wider purpose in social, political, economic, religious, moral evils. He employed this weapon to end all exploitations and differences between rich and the poor, the capital and the labour. It was employed in individual and collective form, nationally and internationally, to solve the problems.

Satyagraha is, thus, offered in respect to those who make no claim to be Satyagrahi. The first and the last work of Satyagraha or Satyagrahi is ever to seek an opportunity for an honourable approach.[43] A Satyagrahi remains always ready for give and take; for a voluntary surrender of Non-essentials.[44] He would never compromise on the basic moral issues involved in the conflict. But the compromises will never be at the cost of the cause or the country. The compromise and its time can only come when both are of one mind on fundamentals.

REFERENCES

1. *Vonoba on Gandhi*, Translated by J. P. Uniyal, p. 9.
2. Gandhi, M. K., *Hind Swaraj*, p. 65.
3. Gandhi, M. K., *Young India*, II, p. 821.
4. Gandhi, M. K., *Harijan*, 24.06.1939, p. 174.
5. Gandhi, M. K., *Harijan*, September 24, 1934.
6. Shukla, C., *Conversations of Gandhi*, p. 41.
7. Gandhi, M. K., *Harijan*, September 1, 1940.
8. Gandhi, M. K., *Harijan*, October 23, 1937.
9. Gandhi, M. K., *Young India*, November 3, 1927.
10. Gandhi, M. K., *Young India*, June 18, 1925.
11. Gandhi, M. K., *Satyagraha in South Africa*, pp. 113 to 15.
12. Gandhi, M. K., *Young India*, May 12, 1922, p. 03.
13. Gandhi, M. k., *Satyagraha in South Africa*, pp. 113 to 15.
14. Appadoral, *Documents on Political Thought in Modern India*, p. 319.
15. Gandhi, M. K., *Young India*, II, p. 1183.
16. Gandhi, M. K., *Satyagraha in South Africa*, p. 159.
17. Gandhi, M. K., *Satyagraha in South Africa*, pp. 182-83, 187-88.
18. *The Collected Workes of Mahatma Gandhi*, Vol. xx, p. 84.
19. *The Collected Works of Mahatma Gandhi*, Vol XII, pp. 350-51.
20. Gandhi, M. K., *Harijan*, October 3, 1953, p. 242.
21. Gandhi, M. K., *Harijan*, October 3, 1943, p. 242.
22. Gandhi, M. K., *Harijan*, October 3, 1943, p. 242.
23. Gandhi, M. K., *Satyagraha in South Africa*, p. 285.
24. Gandhi, M. K., *Young India*, March 19, 1925 p. 95.
25. *The Collected Works of Mahatma Gandhi*, Vol XV, pp. 248 to 50.
26. Gandhi, M. K., *Young India*, June 4, 1925, p. 189.
27. Gandhi, M. K., *Harijan*, April 15, 1933, p. 08.
28. Shah, K. and Diwakar, R.R., *Vinoba on Gandhi*, pp. 37-38.
29. Shah, K. and Diwakar, R.R., *Vinoba on Gandhi*, pp. 38-39.
30. Shah, K. and Diwakar, R.R., *Vinoba on Gandhi*, p. 41.
31. Extracts from a Speech on Message of Lord Buddha at Mahania (Shahabad) on 17th May 1954.
32. Appodorai, *Documents on Political Thought in Modern India*, Vol. I, pp. 402-03.
33. Shah, K. and Diwakar, R. R., *Vinoba on Gandhi*, p. 45.
34. Shah, K. and Diwakar, R. R., *Vinoba on Gandhi*, p. 46.
35. Shah, K. and Diwakar, R. R., *Vinoba on Gandhi*, p. 52.
36. Gandhi, M.K., *Young India*, II, p. 1183.
37. Gandhi, M. K., *Harijan*, April 29, 1939, p. 101.
38. Gandhi, M,K,*Harijan*, March 23, 1940, p. 53.
39. Gandhi, M. K., *Young India*, August 8, 1929, p. 263-64.
40. Gandhi, M. K., *Harijan*, December 10, 1926, p. 369.
41. Desai & Gandhi, *The Nations Voice*, p. 235.
42. *The collected Works of Mahatma Gandhi*, Vo. VIII, p. 61.
43. Gandhi, M. K., *Harijan*, June 10, 1939, p. 153.
44. Gandhi, M. K., *Young India*, III, p. 1056.

2

SOURCES OF SATYAGRAHA

The principle of Satyagraha is not originally conceived by Mahatma Gandhi, though he coined the term. He himself honestly observes, I donot claim to have originated any new principle but simply tried in own way to apply the eternal truths to our day to day life.[1] Who ever lived have preached that very law of Satyagraha with more or less vigour. The philosophical concepts and folkways reveals how Gandhi internalized the age old tradition of India and went to the people of India and of the whole world with teachings phrased in terms of the Vedas, and Upnisadic Slokas, with verses from the Gita and with exhortations familiar from time immemorial.

The principle of Satyagraha is not a new doctrine but it is ever founded in its seed form in all the religious anthologies like the *Vedas*, *Upnisads*, The *Ramayana*, The *Gita*, The *Quran* and The *Bible* etc. It was also vogue in the age of Prahalad, Harishchandra, Socrates, Plato, Jesus and Ashoka. Prahlad was the first Satyagrahi who observed it against his father's cruelty. But he does not mean his action as Satyagraha. Same is the case with religious and spiritual actions of Rama, Krishna and other characters of the sacred books of the universe. Even Gandhi himself was unknown about Satyagraha when he started his resolt of passive resistance in South Africa. The principle called Satyagraha came into being, before that name was invented. When it was born, I myself could not say what it was.[2]

Satyagraha means insistence on truth by offering Non-violent resistance to untruth or evil. It is a weapon of winning untruth by truth, violence by Non-violence, hatred by love and evil by good. It is insistence on truth and Non-violence which evolved thousands of year ago before emergence of Gandhi. Gandhi's philosophy of Satyagraha based on truth, non-violence, suffering and the discipline of renunciation, non-attachment, *brahmcharyc,* that he incorporated in his ashram life, are all rooted in tradition.

Vedas

Non-violence and truth, the twin roots of Satyagraha, and the greatest good of all, the goal of Satyagraha are mentioned in the Vedas. The concept of Non-violence firstly appeared as a reaction to the wanton and widespread slaughter of animals in the vedic sacrifices. Later the concept widened in its scope and implication, and by the Sixth Century B. C. became a vital force. In *Rig-Veda* and *Yajurveda* we find glimpses of love and non-violence. Rigvedas emphasises upon Vayam and Aham. Former stands for the greatest good of all or Sarvodaya. In the *Purusha Sukta* of the *Rigveda* it is mentioned that the entire society should be based on four divisions. Each of the divisions should perform the duty without disturbing and changing the duty. These divisions should be based on mutual love and harmoney. Beside *Rigveda*, in *Yajurveda* also we find God pervading the entire world which reveals of the perfect unity and harmony among all living beings. The aphorism 16/3 of *Sukla Yajurveda* reveals that not only human beings but God also should not make violence by killing the living creatures. O God, you are the protector of all living things, do not make violence by killing our all living creatures upon this earth.[3] Here we clearly find the idea of Non-violence.

Upnisads

The doctrines of truth and non-violence are clearly stated in the Upnisads, but the word Satyagraha has been not mentioned. The seed of Satyagraha, truth and Non-violence are lying there in its seed form. The doctrine of Non-violence first finds expression in a mystical passage in *Chandogya Upnishad* 3/17,[4] where five ethical qualities including *Ahimsa* and *Satya* are said to be equivalent to a part of the sacrifice of which the whole life of a man is made an epitome. *Mundukopanishad* advocates that truth alone becomes victorious in the long run. We also find truth depicted in *Tatriyopanishad*, where God has been defined as Truth, Knowledge and Eternity.[5] Here truth has been established as the highest good. God is Truth and Truth is God, which we later find in idealogy of Gandhi. 'Thou Art Thee',[6] mentioned in *Chhandogyaupnishad* 6/442, lucidly teaches the doctrine of non-violence, not only to human beings but also to sub-human being. Besides these 'I am no other than He', mentioned in *Vishnu Puran* 2/

16/23[7] also reveals the virtue of non-violence. These two maxims emphasizes the unity of all lives which leads to the extension of non-violence to all living beings. The virtues of Gandhi, the theory of love and sympathy finds its seeds in these Upnisadic extracts. Before Gandhi the idea of the greatest good of all and love for all living things was lying in its seed form in Upnisadic aphorisms.

Manusmriti and Prasastapada

The ethics and objectives of Hindu thought and practice, the concept of Truth and non-violence has a prominent place. Manusmrti also contains the undeveloped form of truth and Non-violence. In Manu's classification of duties, Satya is listed among the Sadharna Dharma or Common duties. In aphorism Manusmriti 10/63[8] there is clear depiction of truth, non-violence, non-stealing and saucha, the essential qualities of a religion. To be a true religious one should have to follow these qualities. The ten class of common duties enumerated by Manu are.[9]

(i) Steadfastness (*Dhrti*)
(ii) Forgiveness (*Ksama*)
(iii) Application (*Dama*)
(iv) Non-appropriation or Avoidance of Theft (*Cauryabhava*)
(v) Cleanliness (*Saucha*)
(vi) Repression of the Sensibilities and Sensuous appetites (*Indriyanigraha*)
(vii) Wisdom (*Dhi*)
(viii) Learning (*Vidya*)
(ix) Veracity (*Satya*)
(x) Restraint of Anger (*Akrodha*)

In Prasastapada's classification of the duties Satyavacana or 'Speaking of truth' is one of the generic or common duties, common to all stages of life and all varnas or social classes and communities.[10] Here *ahimsa* is a duty not simply in the negative sense of mere cessation from harm or injury, himsabhava, but also in the positive sense of a definite resolve not to hurt a living being, *bhutanam anabhidrohasam kalpah.*[11] Thus in Manusmriti and Prasastapada it has been clearly revealed that to be a true religious satya, *ahimsa* are prerequisite qualities. We also find in Manusmriti that in some cases or condition, violence is also practised to save the religion, *Satya* and *ahimsa.* If teacher, child, old man and a brahmin becomes violent, then in such case they should be killed. This kind of (Violence) killing is not treated as a kind of violence, but it is a kind of non-violence practised in order to protect the religion.[12] Later it was adopted by Gandhi in his theory and practice of non-violence.

Yogasutra

Yogasutra of Patanjali consists of the five *Yamas*[13] and *Niymas*[14]. *Ahimsa, Satya, Asteya, Brahmcharya* and *Aparigraha* are the five cardinal virutes; of these Ahimsa and Satya are of due importance which purifies the mind of the evil passions and clears the ground for *Yoga*. Patanjali lays down that ahimsa is not merely a negative doctrine in the sense of avoidance of violence, but it also implies good will towards all creatures.[15] Gandhi elaborated these cardinal principles and made them an integral part of the discipline of Satyagraha. Patanjali adopted ahimsa in a too much broad sense and established it with saying that as soon as ahimsa is perfected, all enimity around ceases[16]. It is to be cultivated without any exceptions as to particular creatures and without any restrictions to specific occasions or particular methods[17]. Thus ahimsa and truth are the principle basically discussed in *Yogasutra*. We find here ahimsa in its developed form.

Yogasutra also aims good will of all creatures with help of ahimsa and Satya, which clearly indicates the idea of universal good, upliftment and betterment of all contained in it, which was later termed Sarvodaya.

Ramayana

The tradition of *Satya* and *Ahimsa* was further developed in the epic like Ramayana, the guide of Indians form centuries. Both *Ramayanas* of Valmiki and Tulsidas beautifully presents the principle of truth and non-violence. Valmiki painted Ram as God or Truth and established, Truth is God. Truth has been established as the highest duty for all time and place. The Vedas are based upon truth, so truth is no other than God.[18] It gave a clue to the nature of truth that truth is God, which was later established by Gandhi. It also clearly reveals that to give punishment to someone who is liable for it is not violence because violence done for the betterment of others and to maintain Socio-religious dignity is considered as Non-violence which is clear from the aphorism of Valmiki Ramayana.[19] This was also adopted and elaborated by Gandhi.

Tulsi's *Ramayana* also consists of the traditional thought of truth and Non-violence in the deep sense of the term. The fight between Rama and Ravana represents the eternal duel between the two forces good and evil in human psyche. Victory of Rama (the good) over Ravana (the evil) represents in the human heart. In fact it is not the description of what happened thousand of year ago but it is the picture of what is going on in every human heart today. Tulsi's Ramayana thus contains the age old concept of truth and Non-violence in the character of Rama.

Mahabharatha

The *Mahabharata* is not really an earthly war but war in human body and society in which the duel goes on between the good and the evil, truth and untruth, violence and Non-violence, light and darkness, right and wrong. Finally good, truth, Non-violence gains victory. Here also Non-violence and truth has been praised. The *Mahabharata* directly advocates ahimsa, and by the time of the *Mahabharata ahimsa* had became the highest duty. Vyasa extols *Satya, ahimsa* and other Non-violent values at several occasions in the epic. The wounded Bhisma exalted ahimsa in his discourse to Yudhishthira, that Ahimsa is the highest religion, the highest penance. It is the highest truth from which all duty proceeds[20]..

In the Shantiparva, Kapila speaks of ten ways to attain Brahman, Kindness, forgiveness, peacefulness, Non-violence, truth, straightforwardness, absence of pride, modesty, forbearance and tolerance.[21] The hard and the soft yields alike to the soft, infact there is nothing impossible for the soft, hence the soft is more powerful than the hard.[22] Here soft is for Non-violence and hard is for violence, and it has been established that Non-violence is the greatest virtue or duty and it is much powerful than violence.

In the above aphorism of Shantiparva, Kapila speaks of ten way to attain Brahman in which truth is also one of them, like Non-violence truth was also established as the highest duty, the greatest virtue. Non-violence is the highest truth and truth is the soul of Non-violence. Without truth no other virtue can proceed. Truth is the highest religion, highest virtue, highest penance, from which all other virtue proceeds.[23] We find that *Mahabharata* advocates truth and Non-violence as the highest virtue the quality of the god, and thus thousand years before Gandhi, truth and Non-violence was established from where he got it in its developed form.

The Gita

The Gita, the song of the Lord, is a part of the *Mahabharata* and its philosophic background is of the Upnisads. It stands for dharmayuddha, but basically it is a tradition of truth and Non-violence. As a source according to time, the *Gita* comes after *Veda, Upnisad, Ramayana*. But going through its barying interpretations, the Gita occupies the pre-eminent place as a pleader of truth and Non-violence. *The Gita*, like the *Mahabharata*, of which it is the most valued part, is in its deep sense of the term a work on Non-violence and truth. The central teaching of the Gita is Anasakta Karmoyoga the way to self realization. Anasakti transcends *Ahimsa*, and that is why one who would be anasakta (selfless) has necessarily to practice non-violence in order to attain the state of selflessness. *Ahimsa is*, therefore, a necessary preliminary, included in anasakti. Thus *Gita* in its broad and deep sense teaches ahimsa. The result of selfless detachment is uttermost truth and non-violence.

Amongst the depicted characters, Arjuna is an imperfect incarnation violent, surrounded by false notions of pity, oversion, attachment and irreligion. But on the other hand Krishna is a perfect incarnation, above all, perfect and non-violent. The votary of non-violence in *Gita* is called *Sthitaprajna* or *Trigunatita*. In both the second chapter and the last chapter of the *Gita* the author speaks of the *Sthitaprajna*, who enjoys a state of blissfulness above all three gunas. He is an apostle of truth and Non-violence, and he is a true Non-violent resister, free from the torments of pleasure, pain, joy, sorrow, anger, hatred, attachment etc. The Character of a *Niskamkarma Yogi* is of a true Non-violent resister who has strong insistance upon truth. Thus the supreme state of detachment can be achieved only by insisting on truth and the practice of Non-violence. A person of perfect mental equilibrium risen above violence, a true practicener of Non-violence, can or make violence for the good of all without the least attachment, can be Non-violent even while killing.[24] For the ordinary mortal treading this solid earth the practice of ahimsa is essential for achievement of the state of Non-attachment. In the sixteenth chapter of the Gita we find description of Non-violence, purity of heart, fearlessness, truth etc in aphorism, 1, 2 & 3. Here Krishna says to Arjuna about Non-violence that never hurt, harm or give injury to any living being human or subhuman due to anger, calumny, fickleness. Also one should not assist to any such person who harms others. In other words, one should remain Non-violent in thought, words and deeds. Fearlessness, Purity of heart, control of senses, non-injury, truth, absence of anger, renunciation, tranquility, absence of calumny, gentleness, modesty, absence of fickleness, forgiveness, absence of hatred are the qualities of person who attains the stage of Non-attachment, says Krishna.[25] In the 5th aphorism of Chapter ten also we find truth, fearlessness etc., that these are the qualities of the Blessed Lord and also of a man who attains *Sthitaprajna*.

Gandhi later adopted the concept and practice of Anasakti and made it the quality of a Satyagrahi. *A Niskamkarma Yogi* is a true Satyagrahi because he is the true insiter on truth and Non-violent resistant which was later termed Satyagraha. The idea of duty contained in the *Gita* also shared in formation of Gandhian idea of civil resistance. The key to Gandhi's theory and practice is that no secrifice is great for the upkeeping of rightness, said in the Gita. Thus the votary of truth and Non-violence, called *Sthitaprajna* in the Gita is called Satyagrahi by Gandhi.

Jaina Philosophy or Arhat Darshan

Jaina philosophy or the *Arhat Darshan* is also the chief propogator of truth and Non-violence. Non-violence infact the leading tenet of Jaina philosophy. Though the jainas are not the originators of the Ahimsa doctrine, yet it glorified ahimsa as the core of their thought and practice. According to Jainism the way to salvation lies through three *jewels* (Triratna); *Jnana* (Knowledge of reality as it is), *Sraddha* (faith in the teachings of the Jainas), *Caritra* (Cessation from doing all that is evil). This Caritra consists of five great vows (Pãnchmabavratha); *ahimsa* (not taking any life even by mistake or unmindfulness), *Sunarta* or *Satya* (Speaking in such a way is true, good and pleasing), *asteya* (not taking anything which has not been given), *Brahmacharya* (abandoning lust for all kinds of objects, in mind, speech and body) and *Aparigraha* (abandoning attachment for all things). These all right conduct and five great virtues has been described in Arhat or Jaina Darshan.[26] In aphorism 22 of Arhat Darshan, we find explanation of Non-violence in five senses. If one avoid the killing of human beings, birds and animals, and plants in even pramad, such kind of vow is called real ahimsa. *Ahimsa* according to Jaina is of five senses.[27]

(i) To protect soul from sensual pleasure.
(ii) To protect one's own self with help of mind.
(iii) To walk carefully in order to protect living beings from killing.

(iv) To walk across or to accept different postures after careful survey and effort.

(v) To take food or drink water carefully.

Thus is Jaina thought and practices, the stress is laid upon the virtues of ahimsa, Sunrta or Satya, asteya and brahmacharya, but the root of all these is *ahimsa. Sunrta, asteya* and *brahmacharya* are made to follow directly as secondary corollaries of ahimsa. *Ahimsa* may thus be generalised as the fundamental ethical virtue of Jainism. Judgement on all actions may be passed in accordance with the standard of ahimsa, sunrta, asteya and brahmacharya are regarded as virtues, as their transgression leads to *hinsa.*[28] The Jaina doctrine of ahimsa is infact an extreme application of a great sovereign truth. Gandhi's opinion that a Satyagrahi should not destroy even the smallest insects and he should observe Non-violence in thought, words and deeds, clearly reveals the fact that the seeds of Satyagraha is in Jaina philosophy. He included the virtues of Jainism in the vows of Satyagrahi. Gandhi only took into account the positive aspect of ahimsa, whereas Jaina's had the extreme application of the negative aspect as well as positive of the vital principle ahimsa and its secondary corollaries.

Buddhism

Buddhism avoids the extreme application of the vital principle ahimsa, taken by Jainism. It was infact a revolt against the hardend formalism of Brahmanical tradition, which left a age old mark on the culture of India. Buddha performed social and philonthropic services. He took love not as a social or personal virtue but a universal virtue. He believed in the unity of all living beings which is possible if one and all practices Non-violence in thought, words and deeds. The basic tenets of Buddhism are universally known, which includes the doctrine of the Middle Path (avoidance of extremas); Non-violence; Non-hatred; friendliness to all; renunciation; continence; and the ideal or reaching nirvana, freedom from the cycle of births. Buddha emphasized the importance of the qualities of *avera* (Non-hatred) and *Karuna* (Compassion) which forms the philosophical foundations of the concept of Non-violence. Here Non-violence does not mean mere not killing but it is a positive doctrine which includes all constructive and reformative actions. The Aryan Eight fold way, the moral code of self-decipline is the very essence of Buddhism. It is a gospel of self-mastery meant for them who forsake the dark state of life in the world.

The way rejects the two extremes of self mortification and self indulgence is essentially Non-violent. *Ahimsa* is the first among the ten percepts for the order (Sikhapadani) and among the five rules of conduct for laymen (Panchasilani).

The Buddha teaches ahimsa both as love and avoidance of injury to self and others. Ahimsa finds its expression in love, pity, tenderness and impartiality (meta, karuna, mudita and upekha). The love that the Buddha teaches is the deliberately radiated well wishing love towards all living things. This love is unsullied by motives of sense desire, passion or hope of a return. The Metta Sutta brings out clearly the Buddha's ideal of ahimsa that as a mother, even at the risk of her own life, protects her son, so let there be goodwill without measure among all beings. Let goodwill without measure prevail in the world, above, below, around, unstinted, unmixed with any feeling of differing or opposing interests. If a man remain steadfastly in this state of mind all the while he is awaken, there is come to pass the saying.[29] The Buddhas theory of Non-violence is thus not related to the ideal of a social order or to a political system, but it (Non-violence) is confined to personal relations. Non-violence is all the same, his doctrine of avoiding all violence, returning love for hatred and compassion for all life, is in its deep sense one of the greatest steps forward taken by mankind. Men are not the masters of even the lowest creature and crowling things, but trustees because the human being are endowed with love, intellect and other good qualities.

Buddha advocated that the enemies should be converted into friends, and this conversion should be Non-violently. He pleaded for good feelings towards opponents. He preached and practised ahimsa in thought, words and deeds and conceived ahimsa to be a tenet of personal action and motivation. Here it becomes clear that Buddha was himself a great Satyagrahi. The essential teaching of Buddha reveals how the essentials of Satyagraha as conceived in modern times by Gandhi are rooted in Buddhas thought and practices thousand of year before Gandhi. By no warth should he conquer worth; unworth by worth should he overcome; he should overcome the stingy by a gift; by truth him who doth falsely speak.[30]

Satyagraha, a weapon of meeting evil by good, hatred by love, violence by Non-violence, as preached by the Buddha, proves that Gandhi adopted the positive aspect of ahimsa from Buddhism. Like Buddha he too emphasizes the greatest happiness of all or Sarvodaya and inflicted suffering to his soul for removing the suffering of the world. Like Buddha, Gandhi also pleaded for the cultivation of good feelings towards the opponent. What Buddha taught to the whole of the man kind, Gandhi tought to Satyagrahi's. Gandhi adopted the universal virtuous nature of Non-violence from Buddhism. We find a detail explanation of truth and Non-violence in Buddhist thoughts in its complete developed form. Except Jainism, none took the concept of Non-violence to such a great extent like Buddha. Buddha is the symbol of truth and Non-violence in all ages. After Buddha, Gandhi was the real propogator and follower of Buddhist vital principle of truth and Non-violence. Thus, what Gandhi pleaded in the 20th century A.D. was preached by Buddha in the 6th century B.C. Also we do not find any difference between the thoughts of Buddha and Gandhi. Buddha was a Satyagrahi in the age when the term was not coined, which clears that how much old is the concept of Non-violent resistance, which was later called Satyagraha.

Confucianism and Taoism

China, too, has had a long tradition of truth and Non-violence. For thousands of years. Non-violent resistance has been a well known weapon and the principle of disarmament can be traced in China as far back as 546 B.C. The age old Chinese religion Confucianism and Taoism are pacific in their nature, principle and practice.

Confucious (about 551-478 B.C.) strongly advocated and preached truth and Non-violence as the part and parcel of human life. He pleaded Non-violence as the only means to cope with all the evils. He preached that truth is greatest quality, the pre-requisite to practise Non-violence, the greatest of all methods. He strongly pleaded the principle of returning good for evil and proposed to repay injury with justice.[31] In the golden rule of confucious, the basis of all relations was the principle of reciprocity, 'men should not do to others as they donot want done to themselves.[32]' He forbaded the principle of overcoming evil by love. To him an integrated harmonious life is better to mere courageous death. He was in fact the preacher of peace and Non-violence.

On the other hand Lao Tse, a contemporary of Confucious, who has been called 'anarchist, evolutionist, pacifist and moral philosopher', whose teachings later developed into modern Taoism, an advance on Confucianism. He laid emphasis upon the positive aspects of truth and Non-violence on conquering evil by love. Tao itself means the way and Lao Tse says that the highest duty of man is in learning and imitating the Tao, the eternal cosmic principle, the principle of Non-assertion, means self effacement and returning good for evil. the opposite of egotism and violence. Lao Tse enunciated the doctrine of Non-resistance. He was the advocator of Non-violent struggle on the path of peace and harmony. He pleaded to get rid of evil by good, violence by Non-violence etc.

Thus we find that there was not only principle but also practise of Non-violent resistance in China, which we find in form of Gandhian Satyagraha in modern times. In fact Confucious and LaoTse were the real predesors of Gandhian theory of civil resistance or Satyagraha in its principle and practice for one and all.

Christianity

The words of Mahatma Gandhi that the New Testament, especially the 'Sermon on the Mount' awakened him to the rightness and value of Satyagraha, establishes the fact that Jesus and his teachings are an important source of Gandhi's philosophy of satyagraha. Christianity is of Jewish origin, a religion attached to Non-violence. It is nothing but the teaching of the old Testament which prophets the law of love. Jessus makes the law revolutionary and transforming by raising it from the level of Non-retaliation and creative purpose.[33] Jesus, the prince of peace condemned the use of physical force and preached the law of love and Non-resistance.

The teachings of the Christ logically follows from his self principle of love and brotherhood of man and God. Love for him was not a personal, but a collective universal virtue. No other religion says so firmly that God is Love, except the New Testament which is full of the word. He said, love your enemies, bless them that curse you, do good to them that hate you, and pray for them which despitefully use you and persecute you.[34] Jesus thus raises love from the level of natural impulse to that of deliberate intention.[35] We find the supreme instance, the model of non-violent resistance in Jesus on the cross as he prays, 'Father, forgive them for they donot know what they do.' The cross is the symbol of non-violent retaliation or resistance; a powerful and wonderful way of suffering for truth, of gaining victory by good over evil and hatred by love. He preached love, non-violence and compassion for all living beings. The virtues of mercy, non-violence, love, and truth in any man can be truly tested only when they are pitted against ruthlessness violence, hate and untruth, Jesus preached 'Resist not him that is evil,' 'Resist not evil,' and 'Do not resist evil by violence'. Here 'Resist not evil' means evil in not be repelled by evil, but by good. Physical force is to be opposed, not by its like but by soul force.[36]

Gandhi withdrew the concept of God and truth from Christs teaching of non-violence which follows from his faith in the loving of fatherhood of God and brotherhood of man. The Socio-economic and Philosophical extension of Non-violence was firstly introduced by Jesus, which Gandhi adopted in his thought and practices of Civil-resistance. Equality and Non-possession was preached by Christ for first time in Social sphare. His fatherhood of God and brotherhood of man followed by Non-violence became corner stone of Gandhian thought. Jesus was the real ancestor of Gandhian Satyagraha and that is why he is called the greatest teacher of humanity, the prince of Satyagrahi's, the noblest and the best forarunner of Gandhi[37]. Gandhi simply interpreted those thoughts and practices among the mass in vernacular and tried to get adopt the teachings of Jesus in one and all.

Islam

Non-violence and truth is not the peculiarity of any one race, creed or country. Being and expression of Love, it is a universal virtue. Islam like Jainism, Buddhism, Taoism and Christianity, preached the vital principle of love and brotherhood. The message of Prophet is of kindness, peace and love, but love not only for human beings but also for sub-human creations. The *Holy Quran* prefers Non-violence to violence. The very word Islam means peace, safety and salvation. The common Muslim Salutation 'As Salamalaikum' means 'Peace be on you'. Prophet was more modest than a virgin behind his curtain.[38] He said that there is no beast on earth nor bird which flieth with its wings, but same is a people like unto you mankind. Unto the Lord shall they return.[39] We find passages in the *Quran* which reveals that he considered Non-violence, a better technique of conquering evil than violence. He preached to turn aside evil with that which is good.[40] He taught the method of preaching[41] and also taught the principle of religious toleration and the ideal of the universal brotherhood of all humanity without any distinction of race, sect, colour and creed.[42] The superiority of Non-violence over violence has always been preached in the *Quran*. The teachings of the Quran is essentially in favour of Non-violence. Non-violence is enjoyed as a duty where as violence is permitted as a necessity.

Mohammad was prophet of humanity and champion of peace. He preached truth and Non-violence throughout his life for the good of all. The *Quran* permits to fight to those on whom war is made because they are oppressed. It advocates to fight in the way of Allah those who fight against us but without any aggression.[43] The prophet preached persecution as worse than killing.

Prophet Mohammad came upon this earth like Buddha and Jesus, thousand of years before Gandhi, the great religious thinker, social reformer, a philosopher and a messanger of God, who was later followed by Gandhi to each and every foot step in this thought, wards and deeds as the greatest social reformer ever came upon this earth. Gandhi has never for a moment separated the political from the Spiritual, or failed to deal directly with the social evils. The Prophet's Supreme, practical instinct as a Reformer, combined with intense faith in God as the sole creator and director of the universe, has been the constant strength and support to Gandhi. He found the teachings of the prophet of Islam fully compatible with the Principle of *ahimsa* or non-violence.

Apart from all great and small books and religions, religious seers and saints, Gandhi was greatly moved by the thoughts and writings of modern thinkers like Tolstoy, Thoreau and Ruskin. He himself said, that three moderns have left a deep impress on my life, and captivated me. Raychand Bhai by his living contact; Tolstoy by his book; The kingdom of God is within you; and Ruskin by his Unto This Last.[44]

Tolstoy Leo

The teachings of *Gita* depend the compression of Gandhi, but Tolstoy's *The Kingdom of God is within you* gave it a permanent form. Tolstoy developed the concept of Non-violence for the first time in a systamatic manner. Tolstoy gave Non-violence as a positive attribute of love. love for him is not only an internal principle but also an external law of life, the very basis of his principles of Non-resistance and Non-cooperation, which was later adopted by Gandhi in its totality as a technique of Satyagraha. Gandhi adopted the ideal of Tolstoy—'I love others more than I love ourself.'[45] Before Gandhi in modern times, Tolstoy was the great teacher who condemmed the pseudo science of political economy and detested all kinds of violence, because in his opinion all forms of violence are equally wicked.

Tolstoy's philosophy is called Christian anarchism, is in fact the application of the teaching of the Sermon on the Mount to the solution of modern social and political problems. Love is the core of Tolstoy's principle of Non-resistance and Non-cooperation which are identical. According to Tolstoy, the only way to make the world happy is to bring about a condition of the world, where is all beings could love others more than they love themselves.[46] His Non-violence is rooted in the conception that it is a crime to impose one's will on any creature, to force it in any way. Love or the striving of men's soul towards unity and the submissive behaviour to one another that results, represents the highest and indeed the only law of life. Any employment of force is incompatible with love as the highest law of life. If the use of force appears permissible even in a single case, the law itself immediately negatived.[47] Love contains more energy than anger. It is more inclusive as a sentiment and attracts to itself more energies than anger. It involves the very principle and essence of continuity of life itself. Love is more lasting, and if considered as an instrument it can be more efficiently and effectively wielded, has better aim, better falcrum than anger. Love gains a stronger and more lasting approval from the rest of mankind.

To bring co-operation, Tolstoy is against the method of violence. He strongly advocated the method of love, Non-resistance and Non-cooperation. He laid great stress on the moral regeneration of the individual and preaches the dignity of manual work. He showed superiority of moral force over physical forces. He advocated a just and peaceful society in a state free from violence, injustice, inequality, hatred, exploitation and coercion in his book What to do then? He has vehementhy critised modern way of living based upon exploitation and coercion, and introduced two doctrines, Non-possession and Bread labour. He abjured private property and felt aversion for the surplus use of money.

Gandhi was not a through going Tolstoyan, because he was more practical than Tolstoy. Like Tolstoy Gandhi also remained ever ready to adopt his actions to the demands of the changing world. He summed up Tolstoy's teachings in the Indian opinion[48];

(i) In this world man should not accumulate wealth;
(ii) No matter how much evil a person does to us, we should always good to him. Such is the commandment of God and also His law;
(iii) No one should take part in fighting;
(iv) It is sinful to wield political power, as it leads to many of the evils in the world;
(v) Man is born to do his duty to his creator, he should therefore pay more attention to his duties than to his rights; and
(vi) Agriculture is the true occupation of man. It is contrary to divine law to establish large cities and factories so that some would become rich by exploiting the poor.

Thus we find the Gandhi had the penchant for extracting ideas of the great teacher Tolstoy, which appealed to him to his deepest sense of his heart. The cult of peace and non-violence has gathered great strength in the thoughts and works of Tolstoy. Going through the thoughts of Tolstoy we find that he was the real forerunner of Gandhi, who explained Non-violence and love in its brodest sense. The words of Gandhi is itself the evidence that how much he adopted Tolstoyan theory in his principle and practice. Next to the Raychand Bhai, Tolstoy is one of the three moderns who have exerted the greatest spiritual influence upon my life.[49] Gandhi read 'The Kingdom of God is within you,' fifty years ago when he believed in violance and was passing through a stage of Scepticism. At this curse of scepticism, Tolstoyan thought saved him, as he said, the reading of the book cured me of my Scepticism and made me afirm believer in *Ahimsa.*[50] He also considered himself a devoted admirer who owes much in life to him.[51] J.J. Doke portraited Mahatma Gandhi as a true disciple of Tolstoy.[52] Tolstoy's method to made the world happy' by bringing such a condition in the world where in all beings could love others more than they love themselves.[53] This, the law of happiness of Tolstoy became the foundation stone of his magnificent tower of truth and non-violence named Satyagraha.

Thoreau

Henry David Thoreau an American anarchist made no less impact on Mahatma Gandhi in strengthening, widening and confirming his idea of *Satyagraha.* He for the first time used the term Civil-disobedience and employed the technique of non-payment of taxes against the slavery of his country. Gandhi adopted these two principles down to his heart thought, words and deeds. He explained his theory and practices and gave a new shape to principle of Civil-disobedience given by Thoreau. Thoreau applied Civil-disobedience in political sphere only, but Gandhi applied his Civil resistance in all spheres of life. Civil-disobedience of Thoreau became not only a technique but part and parcel of Gandhi's technique of non-violence. Gandhi incorported Thoreau's ideas of the essential goodness of an individual, non-cooperation with unjust, co-operation with just, and shared his view that, 'that government is best which governs the least'. There will never be a free and enlightened state untill the state recognizes the individual as a higher and independent power, from which all its own power and authority are derived, and treats him accordingly.[54]

Thoreau's theory can be summed up as the maximum of co-operation with all people and institutions when they lead towards good and non-cooperation when they promote evil. He justified not only passive but also active (violent) resistance. He belived in man's natural impulses to goodness, argued for the supermacy, under all conditions, of conscience and help up the ideal of a future society without any rule.

The earlier writings of Gandhi,[55] clearly reveals and made easy to draw out the impact of Thoreau's ideas upon Gandhi. A closer study of the relationship between the ideas of Thoreau and Gandhi, done by George Hendrick,[56] clearly marks the Thoreauvian imprint on Gandhi. Gandhi himself acknoledged his indebtness to Thoreau which is known by his appeal 'To American Friends,' you have given me a teacher in Thoreau, who furnished me through his essay on the 'Duty of civil Disobedience' scientific confirmation of my deeds.[57] In the letter writen to Roosevelt on July I, 1942 Gandhi wrote,'I have profited greatly by the writing of Thoreau and Emerson.'[58] Gandhi himself replied on the extremeness of Thoreau's doctrine to Baldwin that 'the essay of Thoreau contained the essence of his political philosophy.[59] Referring to Gandhi's persistent attachment to Thoreau's essay on Civil Disobedience. Fisher write, a curious friendship, this, of Ancient India for young Americans, still in its national swaddling clothes in the family of ages. Yet the Indian peaceful revolution has taken many of its weapon from the minds and lips of Americans. In a very real sense the seeds of Indian practice of truth and Non-violence was planted in America.[60] Webb Miller observed that, Gandhi received back from America what was fundamentally the philosophy of India after it had been distilled and crystallized in the mind of Thoreau.[61] A careful perusal of the 'Indian Opinion' in which on several occasions Gandhi wrote that Civil Disobedience left a deep impression upon me; reveals how deep was this impression. He often referred to Thoreau and urged the heroic example of the American non-conformist and philosophic rebel. He presented in brief outline the main ideas of Thoreau, in Indian opinion saying 'its inclusive logic is unanswerable.'

Thus there is no doubt regarding the appeal of Thoreau's essay which Gandhi at the most critical phase of his life. Thoreau's writings were known to Gandhi during the formative period of the first time parctise of Satyagraha. *From Thoreau and Ruskin*, he wrote, 'I could find out arguments in favour of our thought and practice.

Thoreau's essay not only propounded Civil disobedience, but clarified the potentiality of non-cooperation which was later enlarged by Gandhi as a social technique of action combined with pure non-violent character, because according to Gandhi 'Thoreau was not perhaps an out champion of non-violence.[62] Haridas T. Majumdar revealed the bare fact to whole world that 'Thoreou's teachings are today the mainspring of the Indian Non-violent movement. Thoreau is known to the Americans as the author of the Walden. To Gandhi and India he is known primarily as the another of the immortal essay on Civil Disobedience. America, through Thoreau may be held responsible for the motif of the non-violent resistance in India. Gandhi gave back to America what he received from her by way of Thoreau. The American people can best show their esteem for Gandhi by enshrining Thoreau in their hearts.[63]

Emerson

Apart from Thoreau, Gandhi was acquainted with Emerson as early as 1903. Thoreau's influence upon Gandhi was far greater, but Emerson directly influenced the Mahatma. Thoreau's influence upon Gandhi, may be also credited to Emerson's teachings indirectly.[64] After reading Emerson, Gandhi established that education means character buliding, it means a knowledge of duty, and not a knowledge of letters. The Essay's of Emerson contains the teaching of Indian wisdom in a Western Guru.[65] In Gandhi's preface to Indian Home Rule, we find Emerson to be one of those masters whom 'he endeavoured firmly to follow.' Gandhi's great admiration for Emerson is also clear from the fact that Gandhi was associated with Emerson club in South Africa and also become member of London Emerson Club.[66]

Emerson, a great ethical critic of Society is known as a great American thinker. 'Go put your creed into your deed, never speak with double tongue and the greatest homage one can pay to truth is to use it,' are the thoughts of his ethical individualism. Throughout his thought the world of Emerson was not a society but a collection of individuals.[67] Emerson was a thinker, and his thoughts gave such a great impact upon the Mahatma that he accepted him as his western Guru. Gandhi knew the real sense of education, thought, speach and actions from him. Emerson continued to be Gandhi's favourite all through his life, the man who's thoughts impressed Gandhi to its towering heights next to Thoreau.

Ruskin

Besides Tolstoy, Thoreau and Emerson, Ruskin's *Unto This Last* has also been one of the transforming energy that shaped the thoughts and experiments of the Mahatma. Gandhi learned the dignity of manual labour, the idea that the good of the individual is contained in the good of all. The one that brought about an inteaneous and practical transformation in my life was Unto The Last. I translated it later into Gujrati, entitling it *Sarvodaya* (the Welfare of all).[68] It was this work which inspired him to found phoenix settlement on principles of bread labour and the responsibility of the Community Organization to provide for the physical welfare of the workers. Ruskin's this work brought an instaneous and practical transformation in Gandhi and he arouse with the down, and reduced these principles to practice. He learned three principles:[69]

(i) That the good of the individual is contained in the good of all.
(ii) That a lawyers work has the same value as the barber's in as much as all have the same right of earning their livelihood from their work.
(iii) That a life of labour and the craftman is the life worth living.

Gandhi remarked, the first of these I knew. The second I had dimly realized. The third had never occurred to me. *Unto This Last* made it as clear as daylight for me that the second and the third were contained in the first. I arose with the dawn, ready to reduce these principles to practice.[70]

Both Ruskin and Gandhi preached the supermacy of the spirit and believed in the nobility of human nature. To both, character was mere important than intelligence. In the Gandhian Philosophy, like Ruskin, social regeneration enjoys priority over political reform. Like Ruskin, Gandhi exhorted the employers to adopt a wise paternal or fraternal attitude towards the working people. Ruskin's impact upon Gandhi was in no sense total,[71] but his ideas on political economy was assimilated by him into his thinking, and adopted the functional view of property without any qualification.

Like Ruskin, he opposed on moral grounds of the Benthamite doctrine that man's duty lies in promoting the greatest good of the greates number. He said that real dignified doctrine is the greatest good of all, *Sarvodaya*. The doctrine of Sarvodaya, the upliftment of all was in its principle form present in Ruskins thoughts. Ruskin was not only the forerunner but the real decorator of the idea of good of all. The resembles of Gandhi with Ruskin also clears that to what extent Gandhi got a great influence from Ruskin. Ruskin's thoughts that the supermacy of the spirit and trust in the nobleness of human nature, and also human character is more important than intelligence; is adopted by Gandhi in his thoughts and deeds.

Gandhi's argument to moralize politics and economics was infact basic thought of Ruskin. Ruskin gave emphasis upon man because man is for him not only a physical entity but a spiritual one. He condemned violence in each and every walks of life. He was against social, political and economic evils, and tried to attain ideal society and state. He pleaded for a new social order, a society free from violence, coercion and exploitation. These all principles were adopted on its totality by Gandhi. Ruskin was in fact the father of the doctrine of upliftment of all, and Gandhi was simply a mere interpreter. All the Socio-political reforms of Gandhi were guided by the vital principles of Ruskin. He drived his principles of moral regeneration of man; moralization of politics and economics from Ruskins thought and ideas.

Ruskin was thus the greatest ideal of Gandhi, not the only but one of the greatest of all predecessors of his thoughts and experiments. Ruskin is in fact the ideal of the Mahatma's Satyagrahi's like Jesus, who is the prince of Satyagrahi's. Ruskin never used the terms truth and Non-violence explicitly, but inspite of that the book *Unto This Last* brought a mervellous transformation in life and thoughts of the Mahatma.

Besides all the great and small religions, thinkers, seers and saints, Mahatma Gandhi derived his notion from Indian culture and tradition, especially Vaishnavite faith. Raichand, Chaitanyadeo and Narsimehta of Gujarat who deepend, widened and strengthened his religious convictions. The eminent personalities like Harishchandra and Shravana gave a impct of great heights, by practising Satyagraha year's before Gandhi. Their stories sparked in him the idea of truth and Non-violence. Ashokas practise of positive Non-violence and peace thousands of years before emergence of Gandhi proved that truth and Non-violence is not a new concept but an age old principle, regenovated by Gandhi in its widest sense. All the great men and women's of Indian tradition contributed a lot in developing the principle of truth and Non-violence, which got its heights in writings of Gandhi.

During his stay in England, he found a people vibrant with energy. He was delighted to find out the civic awareness of the English people.

From my observation of the west, and practicularly of England, I have learned two outstanding facts' Cleanliness and Energy. These energy would prove a great blessing for me and my country people.[72]

He stayed in England on the days when time was going through a period of intellectual awakening the heyday of liberalism. The individualistic liberalist tradition marked its imprint on his mind. Ideologically, Gandhi stood with one foot in the deep individualistic current of the first half of Europe's nineteenth century and the other in the turbulent nationalistic current of the second half of that century, the two stream merged in him and he endeavoured to achieve the same synthesis in his own thoughts and experiments.[73] Those years in London taught Gandhi three subversive ideas; Natiolism, Democracy and Christianity.[74]

Thus, we can conclude that Gandhi renovated the age old philosophy of Non-violence, Socio-political, economic and religious ideals. His great distinction consists in his researches and experiments in the possibilities of all age old principles in all walks of life, and its application to a large mass movements. He adopted Non-violence and truth as a universal law acting under all circumstances and disregard of it is the surest way to destruction.[75] Satyagraha is infact inseparable from the Non-violent outlook of life. He proved himself a good interpreter and a skilled decorator by interpreting age old thoughts from ancient to modern world with decoration of new terms. He was not father of any of his own principle but mere follower and great teacher who tought to mankind in modern age the thoughts of great one's and proved their applicability and relevancy to the modern context. No doubt Gandhi was great for his art of teaching but he was not profounder. Elements of cooperate activity with its aim at changing the course of the given reality that marked off him from other orthodox nationalist leaders and distinguished his philosophy of action from the traditional way of thinking.

Although Gandhi had his own concepts and ideals that differed from notions of Eastern and Western world, yet as one has to move within the limits imposed upon by history, Gandhi led the mankind for establishment of a free and democratic setup and adopted the appropriate methods that came from the past from East and West. No one can separate himself from history, and Gandhi is no exception to his general universal law. He rose to greatness by moving with and within the history. Gandhi was in real sense of the term rooted in tradition and had at once outstepped its bounds, and there in infact lies the originality of Mahatma Gandhi.

REFERENCES

1. *Harijan*, Gandhi, M. K., March 28, 1936, p. 101
2. *Autobiography*, Gandhi, M. K., p. 239
3. Om Yaamisu Girishant Haste Vibhadyrstave Shiva Girim Taa Kuru Ma Hi om Sih Purusa Jagat. *Sukla Yajurveda* 16/3.
4. Ath Yatpo Danmargvamhimsa Satyavachanimati Taa Asy Dakshinaa,—*Chandyoga Upnishad*, 3/17.
5. Satya Janamanant Brhma—*Tatriyopanishad.*
6. Tatvasme—*Chandyoga Upnishad*, 6/442.
7. Sohum—*Vishnupuran*, 2/16/23/
8. Ahimsa Satyamastya Sauchminindrnigraha Dhirvidha Satamkrodho Dasak Dharmalakshanam, *Manusmirti*, 10/63.
9. Sushil Kumar, *The Ethics of the Hindus*, Maitra, University of Calcutta, 1963, p. 08.

10. & 11. Sushil Kumar, *The Ethics of the Hindus*, Maitra, University of Calcutta, 1963, pp. 10-11.

12. Guru Ma Balvridha wa Brahma Wa Vipidhitam Attainamayantan Hanyadeva Vicharayan—*Manusmirti* 8/350.
13. Ahimsa Satyasteta Brahmcharyaparigraha Yamah - *Yogastura*, 2/29-45.
14. *Saucha* Santosh Tap Saudhyaedhareprani Dhanene Niyamah, *Yogasutra*, 2/29-45.
15. Maitra, S. K., *The Ethics of the Hindus*, Calcutta University, 1963 p. 220-21.
16. Ahimsa Pratistaya Tatsnidho Vairtyagh - *Yogasutra*, 2/29-45.
17. Maitra, S. K., *The Ethics of the Hindus*, Calcutta University,1963 p. 211.
18. Satyameosare loke satya dharma sadasrita satyabhutanee samane satyamasti per padam dutrmastan huta chew taptane ch tapsexn ch veda satya pratistha nastsyatsyatsyapro valmiki ramayna—*Adyodhyananda*, 109/13-14.
19. Na santapastavya karya aythartha plavam na vynm bhavta chintya naryatma hari satam vyam bhavdusenu dhabmat krit nischaya dandya patye dand dandyoyschapi dandyate valmiki ramayna—*Kiskindhkanda*, 5/61-62.
20. Ahimsa parmo dharm ahimsa param taph ahimsa param satyam tato dharm pravartat anushssanaparva, , (edited P. P. S. Sastri) C IV, 25.
21. Aanresansy chhma santir ahimsa satyamarjvom adroho natimanasch histicha samstha panthano brahmanswete athe pranotiyat param santiparva (P.P.S. Sastri) CC LV 39-40
22. Mriduna darun hanti mriduna hantyadarunam nasadhyam mriduna kinchit tasmaateekchantar mridu vanaparva (P.P.S. Sastri) XXIV, 30.
23. Satya parmo dharm satya param tap satya param satyam tato dharm pravartate shantiparva (P.P.S. Sastri), CLXXX VIII,61-74.
24. Ysas Nahkrito bhao bodhirsyas na lipyate hatnawe sa immalokan hanti na nibadhyate - *The Gita*, XVIII/17.
25. Ahinsa satyamkrodhotyag santipesunam daya bhuteswaloluptan mardwang harichaplam bhawantee sampad devimvibhagtasya bharat—*The Gita*, XVI/2 & 3.
26. Ahimsa sunritastay brahmacharya parigraha—*Arhat Darshan* -21.
27. Na yatpramaoyogen Jativiataty paropanam chrana Sthawarana cha tadhimsa varta matam–*Arhat Darshan*-22.

3

TECHNIQUES (FORMS) OF SATYAGRAHA

The conception of Satyagraha in Philosophy of Mahatma Gandhi is not a doctrine but a method or technique of curbing society from Socio-political evils. This technique or method is not a single faced but diversified. Satyagraha is completely and absolutely void of Non-cooperation, Civil disobedience, fasting etc. are not included with it. In fact these are the steps of Satyagraha; which may be also called as forms of Satyagraha. These steps make it a strong and perfect weapon for fighting against Socio-political evils, which leads to a new kind of philosophical approach and outlook. The present chapter analyses these forms and I am intended to try and find out the basic vision of Mahatma Gandhi regarding the different forms of Satyagraha.

Non-Cooperation

Non-cooperation, is the foremost step of Satyagraha, a Non-violent means and the expression of anguished love, not a negative conception because it always inhers co-operation. Gandhi himself terms it as a means to secure the co-operation of the opponent with truth and justice. He remarks that behind my Non-cooperation there is always the keenest desire to co-operate with the worst of opponents.[1] It is not a passive state but an intensely active, more active than physical resistance or violence.[2] Non-cooperation with evil is much a duty as cooperation with good. It is a protest against an unwitting and unwilling participation in evil. In other words, every God fearing or self respecting man/women must Non-cooperate or dissociate himself or herself from evil in total disregard of consequences. Non-cooperation means withdrawal of cooperation from the state by the people because the state has become carrupt. Non-cooperation is in fact a prelude with cooperation. Once the evil or the abuse is removed, the people can cooperate. Infact non-cooperation is with methods and systems but never with man. It is with the evil in the man but not with man himself.[3]

The idea that underlies non-cooperation is that even the evil doer doesnot succeed in his purpose without carrying the victim with him, and it is the duty of a Satyagrahi to suffer from the results of resistance and not to yield to the will of the tyrant. It is in fact a cleansing process, which amounts to a kind of refusal on the part of the exploited against exploitation. It is a clean harmless and effective instrument, and its intensity depends upon the capability of sacrifice. The right motto should be never one in his injustice. Being non-violent it is neither punitive nor vindicative, nor based upon malice ill will and hatred, but in an active states it is much effective and active.

Non-cooperation predominantly implies withdrawing of cooperation from the state that in the Non-cooperator's view become corrupt. It is a universal remedy applicable to all spheres of human life. By its very nature Non-cooperation is to its least open to children of understanding and also can be safely practised by the masses. It includes all Non-violent resistance for the vindication of truth. If a father does an injustice, it the childrens can Non-cooperate by leaving the parental roof. If the headmaster of a school conducts his school on an immoral basis, the pupils can Non-cooperate by leaving the school. If the chairman of a corporation in corrupt, the members thereof must wash their hands clean of his corruption by withdrawing from it. If a Government does a grave injustice, the subjects must withdraw co-operation wholly or partially to wean the ruler or Government. Gandhi further extended its scope and recomended that armed invasion can also be resisted Non-violently which would be an act of Non-cooperation with the aggressor by demanding and demonstrating, because Satyagraha is not tied up with the military techniques. But in all cases there remains an element of suffering whether mental or physical. When a friend gives up another and a servant his master, they practise a mild variety of Non-cooperation. But the evil doer cannot do without the Satyagrahi's cooperation, Non-cooperation assumes a drastic form. The drastic type of Non-cooperation causes inconvenience and harmful to the opponent. But being conversion as object and love as weapon, drastic Non-cooperation can be adopted on grave issues. The Satyagrahi seeks truth by imposing suffering on himself and not upon others.

Non-violence is the most vital and integral part of non-cooperation.

one may fail in everything else but still continue the battle if one remains non-violent. Violence in one's part proves token of stupidity, ignorance and importent rage. To exercise restraint under the gravest provocation is the trust mark of soldiership. In it, the Satyagrahi makes such a plea that makes the opponent feel that he has a friend in the former. He also tries to reach and capture the opponents heart by rendering humanitarian service whenever and whereever possible.

The methods besides non-cooperation which has been tried to cure evils are—

(i) Those based on the principle of reform.
(ii) Those based on the principle of violence.

These methods failed because either they were half measures or are unsound measures, in fact no measure at all. Reforms fails because they are bound to fail. It is because it imply a compromise and cooperation with the principle of evil. The methods of violence not only proves futile but produces opposite to what they are intended to produce. In it the chain of violence lengthens and strengthens. These methods proved wrong because it overlooks the fundamental facts evil cannot be overcomed by evil, it ceases only through good. These two methods fail because both the two deals with the superficial symptoms only and does not touch the root of the evil, the disease itself. The only way to cure a disease is to remove the causes. For it the thing to do is the purification of one's own self, the means to cease oneself from participating indirectly with the evil. Self-purification and not violence or reform is the real remedy. And to purify one's own self is possible only by withdrawing cooperation. Self is pure when one donot cooperatte with the evil. Non-cooperation with the evil means a closer cooperation among the people themselves. Non-cooperation, therefore, is a process of evolution, aptly called Evolutionary Revolution. It is not like allopathic treatment, but like homeopathic treatment. It is so because the effect of non-cooperation is more certain like the effect of homoeopathic medicine, slow but steady and permanent.

As a weapon, non-cooperation is applicable not only against unjust and improper government, but also against all unjust and unfair authorities and institutions. People can non-cooperate with their unjust government as freely as a son dissociates his cruel father. It is a right recognized from times immemorial of the subjects to refuse to assist the ruler who misrules.[4] For Gandhi non-cooperation, inspite of a part of his creed, it was a prelude to cooperations. Being a means not something negative, a means to secure cooperation with the opponent (evildoer), it contains the keenest desire to cooperate with the worst of its opponents.

But Gandhi advocated non-cooperation only as a means to secure the cooperation with truth and justice. It is a way to attain self-perfection and purification because non-cooperation in itself, the way adopted by Gandhi which made him Mahatma. The chief motto of non-cooperation except purification is to get rid of the feeling of helplessness by being independent to govern one's own self in all possible affairs, and fulfilling both the object to refrain from promoting or doing any violence to individual or property. Non-cooperation is in fact an education which develops and crystalizes public opinion and when it gets organized enough for effective action it attains its goal. It is such an effective method, an active strong and extreme method which is applicable anywhere and everywhere by male and female; old, young and children alike, because in its totality it is an expression of anguished love. But along with its universal applicability, the precondition in application of non-cooperation is that one must not resort to it until one has tried the other forms of Satyagraha. But the best way of removing the fear and criticism of non-cooperation, is to elaborate more fully the scheme of non-cooperation, said Mahatma Gandhi.[5]

Non-cooperation has certain definite stages. Among these progressive stages four are primary stages and rest all are secondary. But the secondary one's are also equally important like the former. The very last stage also cannot be treated as the least one.

(i) The first is giving up of titles of honour and resignation from honorary posts and offices. If there is no response or the response received is not effective, recourse will be to the second stage. This is the mild form of non-cooperation and is the first stage in the movement;

(ii) The second stage includes much previous arrangements—calling out of Government servants. But not a singal servant will be called out unless he is either capable of supporting himself or his dependents or some one else is able to bear the burden. All the classes of servant are not called out at once and not any pressure upon anyone to detach from government service. This stage must be entirely succesaful, if the response is at all on a adequate scale;

(iii) The third stage includes the withdrawal of the police and the military, which is a distant goal of non-cooparation. This is

Hartal

Hartal, different from strike is a technique, a way to practice non-cooperation. It means a general cessation of work in a particular place or throughout the country as a mark of protest against particular act or policy of an institution or a government. *Hartal*, as advocated by Gandhi, is different from now-a-days strikes and *gheraos*. It is in fact a spiritual weapon of business grivances, voluntary closer of shop and suspension of business, usually for a period of 24 hours. Hardly it is observed for a day or for a few days. It is not to be continued indefinitely. It is an external expression and representation of society's disapproval of unwarranted imposition of unjust laws and orders.

But there is a clear distinction between *hartal* and civil disobedience. Hartal is in fact designed to strike the imagination of the people and the government.[9] Hartal is a device through which satyagrahi try to know the reactions of the public against particular act or policy of the Government. It is proper indication to the leaders to what extent they are able to carry on the civil disobedience. Hartal is meant to feel the pulse of the people regarding their readiness to support a particular cause.

Hartal is to be organised in a systamatic manner. The hartali's or the social workers shall undertake the task of education the people and emphasize the need for observing hartal one particular day as a mark of protest, a day prior to the hartal. Education about hartal is necessary because peaceful hartals are not possible if the people are not properly educated about the nature and objective of hartal. The successful hartal is one which is spontaneous and peaceful.

But the application of hartal as a way for non-cooperation is employed very rare because it often proves fruitless and ineffective. Gandhi laid down certain limitations in the operation of hartals.

(i) There should be no hartal without a genuine cause.

(ii) Political hartals should not be mixed up with economic or social hartals. Political hartals have a definite place in non-violent action.

(iii) The sectional organization and unions should not paralyse the life of the whole nation on the day of hartal. If the national reganization with its membership extending to all the sections of the society which alone has the right to give call for national *hartal.*[10] Thus hartal being a form of non-cooperation should be purely non-violent and absolutely voluntary in nature.

Peaceful Picketing

Peaceful Picketing, is another way to practise non-cooperation, a non-violent technique to put up social, economic and political pressure upon the opponent to create political consciousness and spirit of *Swadeshi,* always persuasive and never coercive. Picketing in its inharent nature aims to attain peace by persuading and converting the wrong doer or the opponent without any application of violence. Its aim is to protect against certain evils or abuses. Speech is the only weapon and way of picketing, to be used gently and inoffensively, because the pickets are like the watchman. It has also a great educative value.

Picketing is quite different from dharna because *dharna* is a form of passive resistance, while on the other hand picketing is not a passive resistance. Former is violent in its spirit while later is non-violent. *Dharna* is infact a coercive method of social restraint, a kind of barbarity because it is a crude way of using violence. Gandhi considered dharna worse than violence because if one fight with the opponent, he atleast enable the opponent to return the blow. But when one challenge to walkover the Satyagraha knowing that he will not, we place him in a most awkward and humiliating position.[11] So, Gandhi discouraged picketing in the sense of dharna. He desired that the social workers can take up more systematic education of the these article. Gandhi laid down certain rules to conduct picketing.

(i) At least ten women are necessary to conduct picketing, and one of them is to be chosen as a leader;
(ii) The first step in picketing is to go in a deputation to the dealers and to appeal to them to desist from carrying on such business. The dealers must be presented with leaflets which should explain the evils of such business;
(iii) If the dealers refuse to suspend such business, the picketers should assemble near the shops. Leaving the passage free for movement, volunteers should appeal to the customers to desist from such practices. They should neither form cordons nor obstruct traffic;
(iv) They should carry the banners and boards displaying the appeal in bold letters against indulging in such practices;
(v) They should be in uniform to distinguish themselves from others in such places;
(vi) They should sing at intervale suitable slogans and songs concerning picketed articles;

(vii) They should neither coercee the dealers and the customers nor use offensive language against them. They must conduct themselves in a polite manner;

(viii) They should appeal to the head and the heart of the dealers as well as of the customers but should never create fear among them. They should try to win them over through sincere appeals, convincing leaflets and awakened public opinion;

(ix) They should collect information about the buyers and go to their houses to convince them about the evil effects. They must give a patient hearing to the buyers and sellers and try to understand their problems;

(x) They must have adequate literature to distribute among the buyers; and

(xi) They should maintain diary, record the progress and failures of picketing and try to find out the ways and means to overcome those failures.

Picketing can be organized against any social, political or economic evil or abuse. But Gandhi confined picketing mainly to liquor and foreign cloths. He advocated that picketing would get much force if it should be led by a women and so he wanted women to take part as a leading roles in organizing picketing. Picketing thus is a non-violent means, which strictly avoids violence, intimidation, discourtesy and hunger strikes.

Social Ostracism

Social Ostracism is much more a liable to abuse than strike and hartal. Ostracism is violent or peaceful according to manner in which it is practised. In social life it is impossible to avoid Ostracism extent. It is used against backlags in a community who defy public opinion. But it is used exceptionally in a very limited sense and extent. Non-violent Ostracism is restored in such cases when a defiant minority refuses to bend to the majority not out of any regard for principle, but from sheer defence or worse. It is found effective when it is not felt as a punishment and accepted as a measure of discipline. In its practice, social Ostracism must be non-violent, civilized and not savour of inhumanity.

Gandhi very clearly explained social Ostracism saying that social boycott must not mean depriving a person of indispensable social services, stopping one's food and cloth, depriving one from social and medical services, because to do so would amount to violence. It should be completely peaceful and non-violent. We find no violence if one defies strong clear public opinion on vital matters, denies social amenities and previlages as against social services. Thus in its limited but deep sense social Ostracism should be employed on rare, well defined and justified occassions. One who employs Ostracism in each and every case, takes it at his own risk.[12]

Civil Disobedience

Civil Disobedience is the logical conclusion the last stage and the most drastic form of non-cooperation 'a complete, effective and bloodless substitute of armed revolt'. The earlier stages of non-cooperation are a preparation for it. Civil Disobedience is a rebellion without the element of violence in it. Civil Disobedience is civil breach of unmoral laws. A civil resister simply ignores the authority of the state. For instance he may refuse to pay taxes, refuses to recognize authority of the state. It is also known in the sense of violation of any law as a mark of protest against the unjust government. It means one's desire to surrender to a single unarmed police man. One's triumph consists in being imprisoned for no wrong whatsoever. It is an innovative and all pervative technique of meeting wrong conceived, applied and practises in several situations.

Civil Disobedience is different from criminal disobedience. If disobedience has to be civil, it must be sincere, respectful, restrained, non-violent and never defient. Civil Disobedience doesnot lead to anarchy, whereas criminal disobedience leads to anarchy. Criminal disobedience can be removed by dint of force but such is not the case with Civil Disobedience because to put down Civil Disobedience is to imprison conscience. A civil resister without any violent arms is harmless to the state. Gandhi defines Civil-Disobedience as 'the breach of unmoral statutory enactments'. It signifies the resisters outlawry in a civil; non-violent manner. Civil-Disobedience is really synthesis of civility and disobedience, non-violence and resistance. Resistance to bad laws is essential for man's moral growth, while activity is the demand of a stable social order without which man's life and growth are not possible.

Disobedience is in itself destructive and antisocial. But obedience to an immoral law is even worse and can never be a duty. A law to be worthy of obedience must be moral and democratically formulated. Disobedience to immoral laws of the state is really obedience to a higher moral law, the law of truth and justice. Civil Disobedience is in fact an effort to reconcile the demands of freedom and law.

Civil Disobedience is the inherent right to every citizen,[13] which he dare not to give up without ceasing to be a man. It becomes a sacred duty of a citizen against unjust and immoral laws. It is a delicate weapon and should not be restored too lightly or for its own sake. One and all should understand thoroughly the implication of civil disobedience before one and all could be fit for offering it. It aims at the conversion of the adversary and not at his/her harassment, coercion or defeat. It should not be undertaken unless other normal available channels of redress have been tried and exhausted. Its use must be guarded by all conceivable restrictions and provisions should be made against an outbreak of lawlessness. The area and scope should be kept in limit to the barest necessities of the case.

Civil Disobedience is thus a weapon to resist the unjust and immoral laws of the state by disobeying them. It becomes a sacred duty of the citizens when state or Government goes lawless or corrupt. It aims at paralyzing an unjust, immoral or undemocratic govt. Gandhi advocated that it is a birth right which cannot be surrendered without surrender of one's self respect. A citizen who barters with such a state shares its corruption or lawlessness. It is a purest and perfect type of legal constitutional agitation devoid of all sorts of violence and is limited in application.[14]

Civil Disobedience pre-suppose the habit of willing obedience to law without fear of their sanctions. Being a quicker and more drastic remedy, than other stages of non-cooperation, is fraught with greater danger and requires to be practised more coutiously. It can be practised as a last resort and by a selected few in the first instance at any rate. Having the same aim non-cooperation needs complete unanimity; while Civil Disobedience can neither be expected to be nor need be so widespread to be effective. Civil Disobedience is thus the breach of unmoral statutory enactments. It signifies the Satyagrahi's out lawry in a civil non-violent manner. Civility is in fact the demand of a stable social order without which man's life and growth is not possible.

But being a quicker and more drastic form, it is a risky and delicate weapon which should be applied and practised with a greater caution and much sparingly. Its use must be guarded by all conceivable restrictions. Every possible provisions should be made against an out break of violence or lawlessness. Healthy and creative use of Civil-Disobedience gives greater emphasis on the adjective civil than on the sustantive disobedience. Civil is the very opposite to uncivil and violent. Civil Disobedience is freedom, growth and life. Civil in fact strickly means non-violent and so disobedience to be civil must be based upon some well understood principle, without being capricious, without ill-will or hatred. Civility does not means mere outward gentleness of speech cultivated for the occasion, but an inborn gentleness and desire to do the opponent good.[15] Disciplined civil resister, tranquil atmosphere and non-violent atmosphere are the pre-condition to make disobedience to be civil must be preceded by Civil Disobedience. One who knows to offer voluntary and deliberate obedience to even irksome laws only attains their right goal in practise of Civil Disobedience. It demand a rigorous discipline through adequate practice of the constructive programme and to attain non-violent control over the masses. Disobedience to be civil must also be public and made especially known to all *Satyagrahis.* Adequate discipline is laid down as the precondition of Civil Disobedience. The Prime consideration of it is Quality and no doubt it becomes 'a dear comodity'.

Disobedience is to be directed against—

(i) Particular unjust or immoral measures of a state.
(ii) Against the laws of a state in general.

In the former, the object of Civil Disobedience is to compel a government to withdraw all unjust laws and in the later to paralize a corrupt Government and to set up a non-violent state. Civil Disobedience in case if directed against particular wrong or evil, it can be employed without regard to its consequesces to rouse conscience.

But regarding object of Civil Disobedience, either particular of general, the laws and orders to be disobeyed should be get to one or all choice with grand discrimination. The Satyagrahi may disobey the laws which are harmful and not break laws which lay down moral principles. The laws which are neither good nor bad, neither moral nor immoral must be disobeyed by the Satyagrahi. The laws selcted to disobey should be such that the largest number of people can take part in Civil Disobedience. The state authority should be challanged in each and every way without any violence or moral turpitude. The selction of laws to be broken should be made not by each Satyagrahi for himself but by all in one, for all by the leader.

Civil Disobedience as advocated by Mahatma Gandhi is classified into four categories. He draws a clear distinction between:

(a) Individual Civil Disobedience
(b) Mass Civil Disobedience
(c) Offensive Civil Disobedience

(d) Defensive Civil Disobedience

(a) Individual Civil Disobedience is disobedience of orders or laws by a single individual, an ascertained number of group of individuals. Under it, it is only selected individual who disobeys a certain law. the fall of an individual resisters does not effect other individual resistor. He is an independent and is a leader over himself in the field of operation.

(b) Mass Civil Disobedience is a disobedience of orders or laws by the general public. It is one in which the masses as a whole disobey the laws of the government, when the government does not deserve the consent of the people to rule and has lost the confidence of the masses. Mass Civil Disobedience represents Janashakti, power of the people against the Rajshakti, power of the rulers. But to practise a successful mass civil objedience it must fulfil certain condition:

(i) Firstly, the masses must be well trained for non-violent action; and

(ii) Secondly, mass Civil Disobedience must be taken to prevent outbreak of violence. Under mass Civil Disobedience there is need for a leader who directs the movements. He must launch Civil Disobedience movement only after assessing the preparedness of the masses for non-violent action.

A prohibited public meeting where admission is regulated by tickets and to which no unauthorized admission is allowed is an instance of individual Civil Disobedience whereas, a public meeting to which the general public is admitted without any restrictions is an instance of mass Civil Disobedience.

The distinction between mass Civil Disobedience and individual Civil Disobedience is that:

Firstly, in former, the fall of one effects each and every Satyagrahi, whereas in later, everyone is a complete independent unit and one's fall does not affect the others; because in the former one, not one but all with one another is complete.

Secondly, leadership is necessary for mass Civil Disobedience, but in individual Civil Disobedience Civil resister himself remains his own leader.

Thirdly, in mass Civil Disobedience there remains possibility of failure while in individual Civil Disobedience there remained less possibility of failure or going through whole of its theory and practise it can be said that in individual Civil Disobedience failure is not possible.

Lastly, the most important thing to be get counted is that a state government or institution may copewith mass Civil Disobedience but to cope with individual Civil Disobedience is not possible for a state and so no state has yet been found able to cope with Individual Civil Disobedience.

(c) Offensive Civil Disobedience is non-violent, wilful disobedience of laws, whose breach does not involve moral turpitude and undertaken an symbol of revolt against the state. Disregard of laws relating to revenue or regulation of personal conduct is called offensive aggressive Civil Disobedience.

(d) Defensive Civil Disobedience is involuntary non-violent disobedience of laws that are in itself bad and to obey such law would be not consistant with one's self respect. the formation of volunteer corps for peaceful purpose holding public meetings and publication of articles for like purpose, all are instances of defensive form, It is infact violation of only unjust laws. The obedience to such unjust laws is inconsistent with human dignity.

But difference between the two is that 'Offensive Civil Disobedience' should be applied by a Satyagrahi after severest discipline. It is the most dangerous weapon which implies the violation of laws. It should also be practised to set right some inustice when all peaceful means goes in vain. It embrasses and vexus the opponent, what over may be the object of satyagrahi.

But 'Offensive Civil Disobedience' in forced on the Satyagrahi when he is not permitted to prosecute his ordinary peaceful activities or when insult and humiliation and imposed upon him. That is why it cannot be postponded but ever it is welcomed. It is in fact a duty to be done even if the opponent is in difficulty, for an opponent in difficulty may not expect people to obey unjst or humilating laws or order.[16]

Individual Civil Disobedience is a corporate technique when

practised by a group. Also mass Civil Disobedience starts from a small beginning and gradually develops. Civil Disobedience thus can be kept at the top of non-violence if it is limited to one person only and that one being should be most versed in science. Thus the best quality of Civil Disobedience is that it is essentially an individual affair and so long as if there is even one civil resister offering resistance, the Civil Disobedience cannot die and succeeds at last in the end.

Economic Boycott and No Tax Campaign

Boycott is a kind of punishement to those against whom it is applied, introduced by Gandhi as a weapon in social and economic sphere different from Hartal and Strike, in its basic nature, a direct and forceful non-cooperation. It is a way to practise non-cooperation by boycotting government orders, boycott of school, college and official functions.

Economic boycott is the strongest method to non-cooperate or disobey. Civil non-payment of taxes a form of economic boycott is the last stage in Civil Disobedience and it is used when all other doors of non-cooperation and Civil Disobedience become closed. It is fraught with the greatest possibility of violence unless masses are saturated with the principle of non-violence. This is why it has been considered as the last stage which should be tried only after other forms of Satyagraha. Civil non-payment is for those who have been in the habit of paying taxes regularly, understand the reason and virtue of civil non-payment, have acquired the essential non-violent discipline and are prepared to stand with calm resignation, the confiscation of their property.[17] But application of non-payment of taxes over a large area in the initial stages should prove futile. Non-payment of taxes without the necessary self control on the part of the people would prove to be an act of unpardonable mistake. The certain pre-conditions for the practise of civil non-payment of taxes are that the masses should be properly educated in non-violence, self control and discipline. It is the best and the final step in non-cooperation and civil disobedience. When in case of non-payment of taxes government becomes blind and lame because without revenue no government or institution can exist and function.

Hijrat

Hijrat is also one of the method, which means voluntary exile, a form one of collective as well as individual Satyagraha. Gandhi recommends Hijrat to those who feel oppressed and cannot live without lose of self respect in a particular place and lack the strength that comes from true non-violence or the capacity to defand themselves violently.

If Civil Disobedience goes violent and fires the blood lust of the tyrant, its terror and oppression become unbearable can make Satyagrahi angry or week. For such a case Gandhi suggests that one must exile from the tyrant territory. Exile should be self imposed in its character, even at the cost of hearth and home and all other earthly belongings. But such step should not be thought less as a dramatic gesture because a thoughtless and unplanned Hijrat harms and hurts the Satyagrahi's moral being to submit to the wrongdoer that one would accept death or lose of one's self respect.

Fasting

Fasting is the ultimate and the most potent weapon in the armoury of Satyagraha, suffering unto death, the last duty open to the Satyagrahi to perform. It is in fact the most fiery weapon, the effective way for correction and conversion. It is a suffering, self-inflicted, completely different from non-cooperation, which produces passive suffering inflicted by the opponents. It should be taken as the last resort to be applied in case if all other technique proves futile, when all other avenues of redres have been explored. Fasting is to check the violence to purify social and political atmosphere. The goal of fasting is self purification and this self purification is also in some sense a pre-condition for fasting. Without self-purification on the part of a Satyagrahi, a fast cannot become successful. It should always be practised for genuine causes and should be undertaken on rare occasions only be the persons who have previous experience of personal fasting.

An individual becomes eligible to fast if he satisfied certain conditions. He should have love for the opponents and has renounced worldy possessions. He should be free from animal passions should have inner strength and should not attach importance to success. Once Satyagrahi undertakes the fast, he must stick to his decision. Fasting undertaken by integrity with noble purpose purifies one's self and also to those on whose behalf fasting is undertaken. Such fasts appeal to the conscience of the people and influences people towards the right direction.

Fasting is taken as purification for complete self expression, for the attainment of spiritual supermacy over the flesh. It refers to one's mistakes and failings. It is also a great discipline, a powerful and strong factor in one's evolution. It is the highest expression of the prayer of a purified and loving heart, a means to resist injustice and for converting wrong to right. It is an appeal to the wrongdoer's nature with the object of evoking the best in him. Fasting of an individual personality being a great one, exerts a tremedous impact upon public opinion.

Fasting as a technique of influenceing the mass people proves effective due to the fact that the mind of the people is not influenced through words, speeches and writings but only by thing what they understand like suffering. People only understand the language of the heart and fasting being an unselfish action used for public purpose and not for self-purpose is the language of the heart. Thus the best and most acceptable method of mass understanding is fasting.

Fasting is different from hunger strike because fasting is undertaken with preparation and adequate thought. It can be undertaken by those who are physically fit. But physical fitness is not the only qualification for taking a fast. It can be practised by those who along with physical fitness are also morally fit and with a firm faith in God. Fasting in fact is a spiritual weapon addressed to God. It requires in addition to truth and non-violence, confidence and faith that God grants the strength. If there is the slightest impurity in fasting it should be renounced at once. Infinite patience, firm believe and resolve single mindedness of purpose and complete calm are the essentials of fasting. A Satyagrahi who practices fasting must be free from anger, malice and obey the call of his conscience. True fasting generates a silent and unseen force full of requisite strength and purity which pervades all mankind.

But this spiritual weapon cannot be lightly wielded. It can be resorted to on rare occasions by one skilled in the art under expert guidance. Fasting undertaken without previous preparation and adequate thought never be fast of a Satyagrahi, but it becomes hunger strike. Gandhi laid certain pre qualifications of an individual for practice of fasting and also the occassion when it can be adequately resorted to. Mere physical capacity is no qualification for fasting. For fasting a Satyagrahi must possess spiritual fitness and a clear vision. It requires faith because anger, impatience selfishness makes the fasting violent. A Satyagrahi should have the confidence in God along with truth and non-violence. Infinite patience, firm resolve, single mindedness of purpose, complete and perfect calm are the pre-requisite of fasting. Persons those who intends to go for a fast should possess some personal experience of fasts for spiritual purification.

Fasting, though it has a place in individual as well as group, cannot be used correctly and effectivaly by the masses. It can be resorted to only by few selected and qualified individuals. It cannot be undertaken against one's opponent because it will be a kind of violence done by him. It can be resorted to only against one's nearest and dearest solely for his or her goodness. A Satyagrahi should fast only as a final resort when all other avenues of redness have been explored and have failed.[18] Fast should not be against one party, group or individual exclusively, but yet it excludes nobody. It is for the consciance of all.[19] Fast unto death is the last resort of fasting, an integral part of satyagraha, the greatest and the effective one.

The object of fast is always to evoke the best him. Under proper circumstances it is an appeal par excellence,[20] a fiery weapon with its own science. Unscientific experimentation with it is bound to be harmful. It should be taken by him, who is associated with the person against whome he fasts. The latter must be directly connected with the purpose for which the fast in being undertaken. [21]

Fasts undertaken according to the rules governing them are truely non-violent. There is no room for coercion. It plays an important role in maintaining a struggle non-violent and has a recognised place in religious practice. To practice fast with non-violence is to know its true value. It is to bring heaven upon earth. Self suffering is in fact an appeal to one's better nature, as retaliation is to his baser.

Fasting under proper circumstances is an appeal par excellence. Gandhi pleaded with the political minded people to study non-violence and fasting as its extreme manifestation with sympathy and understanding.[22]

Regarding the problem that what are the things that can be taken in the course of fasting, Gandhi advocated that faster can take fruit juice if he doesnot want to depend on his physical endurance. If the fruit juice is to be taken, it should not be more than what is absolutely necessary for the body.[23]

Fasting should not be considered as a form of Satyagraha in the sense of mass resistance. It may be used as a specific weapon in specific circumstances as an adjunct to other forms. Either in individual or in representative Satyagraha this method may be adopted. But the emphasis should always be upon group action. The efficacy of fasting as a method should be related to the fundamental point of developing the self-initative and self-consciousness of the masses and action on a collective level. This may be also practised for self-realization and also for the removal of injustice, for the communal unity and the acts of violence.

But fasting cannot be taken by everyone. Mere physical capacity to take it is no qualification for it. It cannot be used without a living faith in God, and also should neither be a mechanical effort nor a mere imitation. Fasting must come from the depth of one's soul.

Thus fasting though a very patent weapon has necessarily very strict limitations. It is to be taken only by those who have undergone previous training. Judged by my standard, Gandhi says the majority of fasts donot at all come under the category of Satyagraha fasts, they are popularly called hunger strikes, undertaken without previous preparation and adequate thought.[24] Fasting is a great institution in Hinduism and on the whole done the greatest good to Hinduism. In fact there is no real prayer without fasting. Fasting in fact is prayer of a soul in agony. It is the only way in which one can fulfil his vows and also relieve one's own self from the strain of deprivation.

Fast is a part of one's being of every seeker of truth. This was in fact an experiment in *Ahinsa* on a scale perhaps unknown in history.[25] Fast unto death is not a result of loss of faith in non-violence but it is the last seal upon the faith of non-violence. When human ingenuity fails, the votary of ahinsa fasts. This fasting quickens the spirit of prayer. It is in fact a spiritual act addressed to God. The effect of such action, the life of the people is that fasting awakens.

Thus in the bravest course of fasting Satyagrahi is to suffer cheerfully the worst represion and soften the heart of the wrongdoer. There is no place for fraud of falsehood or any kind of untruth in Satyagraha. Joy lies in the resistance, in the fight, in the attempt in the suffering involved and not in the victory itself. The weapon of violence, even if it is atom bomb, becomes useless when it is matched against true non-violence. The idea of self-suffering is of basic importance in Gandhian Philosophy. But Gandhi's emphasis on suffering is not merely due to his intense religious conviction, but it is also due to his correct estimation of human psychology. Satyagraha is like a cart on which if be overloaded, it may give the way; if no men come forward for it will be staranded on the way, but it will not break, but it may take time to reach its destination. Lastly, if more men comes forward, its end will be witnessed soon.

Gandhi, had, however, made a begining. The logic of the situation demands that his steps should be carried forward. But Satyagraha, which is still praised by thinkers and leaders all around, is ignored when the question of its translation into practice arises. Tagore had anticipated that the west will accept Gandhi before the East, for the East has not yet gone through materialism. Gandhi's technique of Satyagraha, for its forms, is not totally suitable for our socio-economic and religious condition, because we people still live in our traditions and not with modernity.

REFERENCES

1. Gandhi, M. K., *Young India*, II, p. 517.
2. Gandhi, M. K., *Young India*, August 25, 1920, p. 02.
3. Patil, S. H., *Gandhi and Swaraj*, p. 140.
4. Gandhi, M.K., *Speaches*, p. 205.
5. Gandhi, M. K., *Young India*, 1919-22, pp. 191-92.
6. Gandhi, M.K.,*Young India*, 1919-22, pp. 191-92.
7. Patil, S.H., *Gandhi and Swaraj*, p. 141.
8. Appadorai, *Political Thought in Modern Times*, Vol. I, p. 311.
9. Gandhi, M.K., *Satyagraha*, Navajivan Publishing House, Ahmedabad, 1951, p. 25.
10. Gandhi, M.K, *Non-violence in Peace War*, Vol.II, 1949, p. 82.
11. Gandhi, M.K. *Satyagraha*, p. 90.
12. Gandhi, M.K., *Young India*, I p. 302.
13. Gandhi, M.K., *My Religion*, Navjivan Publication Ahmedabad, 1951, p. 25.
14. Gandhi, M.K., *Satyagraha*, Navjivan Publication, Ahmedabad, 1951, p. 174.
15. Gandhi, M.K., *Autobiography*, II, p. 345 by Desai, Mahadeo.
16. Gandhi, M.K. *Harijan*, January 6, 1940, p. 404.
17. Gandhi, M.K., *Young India*, I, pp. 947-51.
18. Gandhi, M.K., *Harijan*, April 21, 1946, p. 93.
19. Gandhi, M.K., *Harijan*, January 18, 1948, p. 514.
20. Gandhi, M.K., *Harijan*, July 20, 1942, p.248.
21. Gandhi, M.K., *Harijan*, October 13, 1940, p. 322.
22. Gandhi, M.K., *Harijan*, July 26, 1942, p. 248.
23. Patil, S.H., *Gandhi & Swaraj*, Deep & Deep Publication, 1983 p. 144.
24. Gandhi, M.K., *Harijan*, March 18, 1939, p. 56.
25. Appadurai, *Decuments on Political Thoughts in Modern India*, Vol. I, p. 357.

4

ELEMENTS OF SATYAGRAHA

Mahatma Gandhi learned what he called "Eternal Truth" from the greatest traditional religions and philosophical teachers of the world. He by confronting with doubts tried to justify them with arguments. He selected and confined his own way, out of several traditional teachings those that appealed to him sound and worthy of application to life. This led to a new kind of philosophical outlook with old elements inherent in its ingredients and composition. In present chapter, emphasis is laid on such eternal elements of that very outlook.

Metaphysical Basis

The writings of Gandhi deals simultaneously with the most immediate tactical and political considerations on the one hand and the broadest historical and philosophical generalizations on the other. In Gandhi's thoughts certainly metaphysics and political notions are intertwined.[1] His basic concepts are not formulated in some ivory tower philosophical detachment, but were direct result imanating from his confrontation with real life presenting itself in diverse and varied forms. Mere knowledge about reality without practical applicability to life had no appeal for him. Philosophy without life corresponding is like a body without life said Gandhi.[2]

In him does the statement that the Indian Philosophy is a way of life first and a way of thought next.[3] The devine is not to be found in detachment from the common life, but in discovering in the concrete demands of each particular situation the best way in which to serve humanity. My being creed is service of God and therefore of humanity.[4] One cannot divide social, political and purely religious works into watertight compartments. I do not know any relation apart from human truth is the important name of God. This is why Gandhi made a transformation by preaching 'Truth is God' instead of 'God is Truth' which he had said earlier. God or truth is infact not only the immanent reality but it is also transcendent.[21] He is not only in us but out of us, not only the life of the universe, but also beyond it as its creator, sustainer and Judge.[22]

Gandhi started with the concept of an omnipresent fundamental spiritual reality which could be Sachidananda or Brahman or Rama or Simply truth. The Sat or Truth conceived by Gandhi is not only an ethical category but as an ontological being of highest realm. Truth is not only a value or ideal but is the highest concrete reality. God as truth is the eternally perfect conciousness. This truth according to Gandhi is not only the Supreme existence but also the chit or the highest gnesis and consciousness because there can be no knowledge apart from truth. Truth as an ontological absolute is not the personal God of the theistic religions but nevertheless as a great Vaishnava devotee Gandhi always made prayers to God.

To Gandhi God is both immanent and transcendent, a purely benevolent power. But having no professional philosophical background, Gandhi used philosophical terms not in any technical sense but in his own sense.[23] The world is constantly changing every moment and is therefore unreal. But inspite of constant changing it has a something about it which persists is therefore real. Gandhi called it neither real nor unreal but *Anekantavadi* or *Syadvadi*. But his Syadvada is not the Syadvada of the learned, it is peculiarly his own. He said "I am an advaitist and yet I support dvaitism". He did not use advaita in the sense Sankar used the term, nor did he take into account the Philosophical implication of Syadvada. Gandhi uses advaita in such a way that it advocates some kind of monism. His use of the story of the elephant and the blind men illustrates the viewpoint that all is one, and is spiritual. All the aspects under which the world is known are genuine aspects of it, reconcilable with its unity. He also apart from advaitism like a Vaisnava theist he exclaimed let us dance to the tune of his bansi-lute, and all would be well.[24] On the whole, it will be reasonable to think that Gandhi was a theist a Vaishnava, rather than an advaitist a follower of Sankar.[25] In the words "We are not , He alone "IS",[26] said by Gandhi. Datta finds a very striking parallel to the famous description of God by Whitehead. The similarity between the two lives in their attempts to comprehend in one synthetic sweep the divergent aspect of Godhead and the different religious traditions representing different points of view.[27]

Gandhi was concious about God is not a person, but Truth. His own Law, an Idea, Law Himself. He did not accept God as a personal one. Here we find hard to reconsile the different ways of his thought. May be God has been viewed by him from two aspects, personal and impersonal, said Binay Gopal Roy. The personal aspects presents the phenomenal picture of Divinity. But the real Divinity is to be found only in the impersonal.[28] God is personal to those who need his touch and one can establish a personal communication with him through prayer and purification. He felt the sense of complete surrender to God, humbly sought his guidance and found that his voice had been increasingly audible as the years rolled by.[29] The help of God never fails in the darkest despair or in the most terrible trail. Such a help was to Gandhi, the visible figure of the invisible God. But inspite of language of a theist, Gandhi was complete catholic in his ideas about God. He identifies God with truth, God with love, law, ethics, conscience etc. God is faith oneself multiply to the nth degree.[30] One and all believe in some principle associated with life and identify it that it is one's God. This faith is enough for one and all says Gandhi.[31]

To Gandhi, there is no antithesis between Man and God. The soul is the only reality in man. He believed in absolute oneness of God and of humanity. The great truth, a principle for higher than that of the brotherhood of man, makes one servent of God's creation.[32] He called God *Sat-Chit-Anand*, one who combines in Himself truth knowledge and bliss. Truth is God gave him the satisfaction and he said that to find truth as a God, the only means is love, that is non-violence and so he said God is Love.

Gandhi's thought about the identification of God with truth bears significance upon his philosophy. He fully identified God with truth saying that these two terms are convertible.[33] For him truth is God and there is no way to find truth except the way non-violence. We find a fine distinction between the two statements of Gandhi, "God is Truth" and "Truth is God".

Gandhi after a continuous and relentless search after truth discovered love as the nearest approach to truth. He also found that love has several meaning in the English language and human love in the sense of passion could become a degrading thing. But atheist has no hesitation to deny the existance of God in their passion for discovering truth. This was the cause why Gandhi advocated truth is God instead of God is truth. Gandhi affirmed his position saying that, "I claim to be a votary of truth from my childhood. It was the most natural thing to me. My prayerful search gave me the revealing maxim, truth is God instead of the usual one God is truth. This maxim enables me to see God face to face and pervades every fibre of my being![34]

Dr. P. T. Raju also observed the fine distinction between the two statements. He says that no one a logical can fail to understand the significance of this change from God is Truth to Truth is God because it makes all the difference in the world. Every significant judgement presupposes an existent subject and the judgement is about that subject. In the judgement 'God is Truth' the existence of God is presupposed. This existence may be questioned when truth, the predicate, would have to be referred to a non-existent subject and thus judgement would be without logical significance. But when it is said that God is the same as that truth, the judgement becomes significant and practically amounts to the proof of God.[35]

Dr. D. M. Datta observes that ordinarily such a simple conversion of universal affirmative proposition would be fallacious. But there are exceptions to this rule too. When the subject and the predicate are equal in extent, the simple conversion is permissible. In the same way the transition from God is Truth to Truth is God cannot be objected by the rules of formal logic, since God is taken identical with Truth.[36]

Dr. Joan V. Bondurant comments on this conversion the 'changed creed' that it may have been with Gandhi's deliberate change in the structuring of his theological statements that he consciously allowed for the fear of construction of Satyagraha. This is an example of Gandhi's philosophical formulations following upon his practical experiments and his efforts in applied ehtics.[37]

Prof. N. K. Bose said in his opinion that with this changed creed, Gandhi was enable to accomodate those who looked on Humanity as their God, and for which they were prepared to sacrifice their all. By enthroning truth on the highest pedestal, and thus Gandhi became a true Catholic, and lost all trace of separateness from every other honest man who worshipped God other than his own.[38]

Thus though the interchange of subject and predicate in an identical proposition is logically unimportant, it was a momentous psychological transition of Gandhi. God is Truth reflects the fact that the search of Gandhi started with God. He had no doubt about the existence of God, but later he found that even the people who rejected God were also in the search of the truth. Truth has thus the greatest appeal to mankind and so Gandhi changed his emphasis from God to Truth, which reveals that, Gandhi did not cared for God, if he is truth, anything but the undeniable Reality revealed in man and outside. Truth is God also suggests that Truth should be the object of worship.

It was in fact an expansion of his faith by which he sympathized all as his brothers in faith who tried to follow the common goal of Truth.

This was an expansion of his early faith in God. God have wide range of meanings with different expressions and backgrounds. This was in fact the plea of Gandhi for the inclusion of the atheist within one's religious fold. It was in fact a thin dilution of the faith which Gandhi prepared for sharing with all and Sundry in his public life.[39] It was the dynamo behind the life of powerful activity.

The quest for truth is the hall mark of humanities march towards enlargement of the frontires of knowledge. It involves practical participation in things. The urge for truth made and led him to the vortex of practical action. Apart from conversion or dillution, the practical bearing of the transition was more important for him.

Gandhi said that God to be God must rule the heart and transform it. He must express himself in every smallest act of his victory. The safest course to believe in the moral Government of the world and in the supremacy of the moral law is the law of truth and love.[40] By this practical method of action on a working hypothesis employed in Science, Gandhi increased his faith day by day, working like a scientist on the hypothesis God as Truth and Love ruled the world, by the response to his faith Gandhi strengthened his belief in God. Gandhi's intense and living faith in God gave into our accounts several vital consequences. Firstly, it led to regard the whole universe with all its sentient and insentient creation as the manifestation of God, and to view all life as one. Secondly, if truth is God it follows that everyone who devotes himself to the pursuit of truth can be sure of receiving the backing of cosmic forces in all his actions. Thirdly, if whole life is one, one cannot serve the society without taking part in politics. Gandhi's conception of God as Truth led him to revolutionize life by insisting upon the principles of Truth and Love. This is regarded as the most important and revolutionary contribution to the political thought and action, a product of the conception of God.

Ethical Basis

Truth and non-violence is the pole star of the whole of the philosophy of Gandhi, which comes first among all vows, the moral principle observed and advocated by him. Vows, says Gandhi, are moral discipline absolutely necessary for self realization. There is no religion higher than Truth.[41] True religion and True morality are inseparably bound up with each other.[42] Moral law is synonymous with true religion.

Religion is to morality what water is to seeds. Religion and morality (God and Truth) are identical according to Gandhi. He stressed on this essential moral 'humanistic aspect' of the religion. This religion viewed as a moral influence leans heavily on a humanistic interpretation of ethics.

But religion makes exhortation to love and lead to Sentimental moralism. Gandhi's achievement is that his ethics recognised the Socio-institutional aspect and kept itself free from 'Sentimental Moralism'. In Ethical Religion Gandhi propounded the doctrine that "The eternal laws of morality which are found to be alike in all religions and are, therefore, binding on all. Morality is binding us because it is the eternal and immutable law of nature. It is its own reward. The moral law is independent of our feelings and opinions, but it has its seat in the soul of every man. So, Truth and Non-violence is within ourselves.[43] Man cannot be untruthful, cruel and incontinent and claim to have God on his side.[44] He rejects any religious doctrine that does not appeal to reason and is in conflict with morality.[45] Morality and religion are identical, and these moral (humanistic) aspect of religion secured their survival and growth.[46]

Gandhi's concept of morality breaks with conservatism. True morality doesnot consist in following the true path for ourselves and in fearlessly following it.[47] Thus the moral concept of Gandhi seems to be a re-echo of the Saintly tradition which is deeply rooted in Indian Soil. The highest moral law is that we should work for the good of mankind.[48] No non-voluntary action can be called moral. This consists of two core principles that underline Gandhi's concept of ethics and morality. Firstly, anything that denies the growth of human personality violets truth and creates violence which is immoral. Secondly, service without any self-regarding motive is the essence of moral behaviour.

Truth

Ethical Religion[49] makes an indication of Gandhi's idea about TRUTH. If not taken into account in a metaphysical sense, it seems to mean the moral law or set of laws. Vows are in words of Gandhi a moral discipline absolutely necessary for self realization, source of strength. He differentiated between truth as a vow or means relative truth as percived by finite one's in relation to a particular set of thought and circumstances, and Truth as the summum bonum, the Absolute, Universal, infite truth, that which exists beyond space and time. For Gandhi apart from metaphysical sense, truth as a duty means the duty to obey the moral law, the duty to do one's duty—'a tautology'. This kind of deduction is present in the writings of Gandhi, where truth is made to cover many principles.

Gandhi identifies truth with God in the sense of the Absolute. Truth or Satya which means real existence is the one and the only correct, fully significant name of God. Truth is perfection includes all knowledge (*chit*) and this knowledge is the source of etrnal Bliss (*Ananda*)[50] God is thus known as truth only. He was completely devoted to truth and nothing else.[51] The Sanskrit word Satya means not only truth but also truthfulness. This is an intrinsic connection between truth and truthfulness. Infact regard for truth generates the truthfulness in thought, speech and action. Truthfulness in the sphere of thought means devotion to facts and eagerness to discover the truth of any matter before arriving at any decision. By Series of experiments he discovered that truth is by nature self evident and as soon as one removes the cobwebs of ignorance that Surrounds it, it shines clear.

Truth also requires self analysis and self purification. It cannot be attained if one remains in influence of lust, anger, greed, infatuation, pride and falsehood. Strong morality can only come face to face with truth. The moral purity, the constant effort to keep safe distance from the deadly enemies enables to stick to truthfulness in thought, speech and action. Truthfulness in speech and action is the natural outcome of the truthfulness in thought. Gandhi was internally convinced of the truth of the ancient Indian dictum, "Satyameva Jayate", truth alone prevails. Truth prevails because it has some intrinsic power. Truthfulness in speech and action flows spontaneously from the love. Truth and love are thus inseparable in thoughts of Mahatma Gandhi. From love; follows the ideal vow of truthfulness, "to speak what is true, good and pleasant". Speaking of truth is thus an art which can be perfected by constant effort is each and every sphere of life and can be realized in words and deeds; speech and writings. "Referring to the Sanskrit text that lays down the ideal of truth speaking, "Gandhi says, "the Sanskrit text means that one should speak the truth in gentle language. One better not to speak, if one cannot do so in a gentle way; meaning thereby that there is no truth in a man who cannot control his own tongue".[52]

The entire philosophy of Gandhi is based upon the fact that truth can be only victorious, for truth is that which is, while untruth means non-existance. If untruth does not so much as exist its victory is out of the question. And truth being that which is can never be destroyed.[53] To realize absolute truth, one should hold the relative truth; which is considered as truth.[54] To realize Satya one must be insistence on truth, because devotion to Truth, being true to the light is the road to the realization of the eternal truth. What a pure heart feels at a particular time is truth, by remaining firm on that, undiluted truth can be attained.[55] Truth has a self revealing nature and as the purificatory discipline removes ignorance, truth shines clear. It has reference to all pros and cones of human life. So, search of truth means through service of all, ceaseless effort for regeneration in all spheres of life. Truth also means social relations including political freedom.

Truth rules out prejudice, evasion, secrecy, deception and also exaggeration, supression or modification of reality. It also implies mutual toleration and avoidance of dogmatism and bitterness, bacause truth in this world is always relative and fragmentry. It is a good guide for individual conduct upon others will be an insufferable interference with one's freedom of conscience.[56] Bitterness blurs one's vision and to that extent disables one from seeing even the limited truth. One had better not to speak truth, if one cannot do it gently and truth without non-violence is not truth but untruth. But non-violent truth or gentle speech does not mean hypocrisy or circumlocutory speech. Harsh truth may be uttered courteously and gently, but the world would read hard. To be truthful one must call liar a liar harsh words, but in form of inevitable use.[57]

Gandhi, being a great scientist in the realm of social truth, great because of his choice of problems, methods of solution, the persistence and throughness of search and due to the profoundity of knowledge of the human heart,[58] he made the test of hypothesis on himself. Every one has the right and the capacity to determine truth for himself/ herself, and this essential virtue, the ability to determine truth, separates man from the brute. A higher moral and intellectual equipment is necessary to know and realize the truth, and those who make experiments with truth attains the conclusion that strict preliminary discipline is necessary to qualify a person to make experiments in the spiritual realm. But mere apprehension, accepts and pursue the truth known by developed souls and suffers in a pursuit of truth and donot need to be highly developed.

Search after truth needs an intensly moral life. Constant endeavour, indifference to other interest of life (vairagya) and the vows truth-non-violence, *brahmacharya,* non-stealing, non-possession are indispensible for the realization of truth. Only such people hear the inner voice of conscience in regard to truth, who practise all the vows of truth. Gandhi holds that these observances are deduciable from truth and are meant to subserve.[59]

Truth can be realized only by means of *Ahimsa* (non-violence). Violence which has its roots in divisive propensities like anger, selfishness, lust etc, cannot take us to the goal. Violence arises out of ignorance, which is untruth, non-existence. It means more than merely to do what one believe to be right. It means that do what one believe and not what others believe, to be right. One must depend upon one's own judgement and conscience and develop them. One must abide by the consequences of one's own judgement. Spartt observed that if this is a principal meaning of truth, the value which Gandhi attaches to that doctrine is easily known and understood. This clearly expresses Gandhi's urge for the people to converse and transform themselves, which gives a beautiful picture that the work of the Mahatma of training himself to be fit for the task.[60] For Gandhi, the question of theological belief was not important and he said, "That will do."[61] The important thing for him was that one must be prepared to suffer for the realization of the truth as one conceives. The moral law is independent of one's feelings and opinions, but it has its seat in the soul of every man, for truth within one's own self.

Non-Violence

Closely interwined with the concept of Truth is Ahimsa or Non-violence. Truth and non-violence are so interwined that it is practically impossible to distangle and separate them. The religion of non-violence is not meant merely for the *Rishis* and Saints. It is meant for the common people as well. Non-violence literally means non-injury or non-killing in thought, words and deeds, found in Upnisads, Jainism, Buddhism and Hindu Law advocated by Manu. Jainism set it rigorously saying not to kill or make injury to any form of life in thinking or speaking, and not even causing or permitting others to kill. On the other hand Manu made the principle of Ahimsa elastic, allowing the killing of animals for food and sacrifice, and killing of man for self-defence.

But Gandhi adopted the middle path between the two. He did not accept Manu's concessions because his attitude was like that of Tolstoy. One must aim at the sky if one wants to hit the top of the tree. He said that flesh is enough weak and lay down rules of concession is to sanctify the failings of the flesh by sanction. So Gandhi stucked and strictly adopted the ideal of Non-violence or Ahimsa. He was much closer to Jaina than Manu, but in practice Gandhi went a different path and could not satisfy the high and rigid standards of Jainism. He brought down upon himself the warth and relsuke of the pious Jains and the orthodox Hindus.

Gandhi showed the dilema that the true believer in perfect ahimsa is put into in practical life. Man cannot for a moment live without consciously or unconciously commiting outward *hinsa.* The very fact of living eating, drinking and moving about necessarily involves some hinsa, destruction of life, be it ever so minute.[62] Ahinsa is not merely a negative state of harmlessness but it is also a positive state of love, of doing good even to the evil-doer. But it doesnot helping the evil-doer to continue the wrong or tolerating it by passive acquiensence. On the contrary, love, the active of Ahimsa requires to resist the wrongdoer by dissociating one's own self from the evil doer, even it may offend or injure him physically.[63] Thus ahimsa is completely uttermost selflessness, which means complete freedom for one's body if one desires to realise one's own self Truth. This can be possible, by being completely detached from the body.

Gandhi was a realist, but not such a realist, one who stops the status quo in the name of realism, because he called such realism, half realism. Being a worshipper of complete Truth or Reality, he did not ignore the reality of love in the human heart which was and is the path of human progress. Non-violence is in fact the law of human species. To forget this reality and divine impulse by we people, by thoughtless deeds is to stop the pogress and pave the way to hell upon the earth. One must remain alive and keep alive the divine quality, and try to make it strong by the practice of love and compassion. Struggling for the ideal is all that is given to man, full effort is full victory.

Gandhi says that one's goodness is to be judged by the goodness of the will, because there is nothing unqualified good, but the good will. A votary of Ahimsa, therefore, remains true to one's faith if the spring of one's all action is compassion. If one shuns to the best of his ability, the destruction of the finest creature tries to save it, and thus strives to be free from the deadly coil of *hinsa.* He will be constantly growing in self restraint and compassion, but he can never become entirely free from outward *hinsa.*[64] Truth can be realized only by the means of ahimsa because ahimsa in closely interwined with the concept of truth. Without ahimsa it is not possible to seed and find truth. The both two are such interwined that it is not possible to disentangle and separate them. They are like two sides of a coin, like a smooth unstamped matalic disc. *Ahimsa* is the means and truth is the end. Means must always be within our reach and if one take care of the means, one is bound to reach the end.[65]

Violence on the other hand has its roots in propensities like anger, selfishness etc, which cannot take one to his goal. It is untruth because the thing truth as known to man is relative and never absolute. Violence arises out of the ignorance called untruth. People look at the thing from different angles and conscience is not the same thing for all. Whether an act is an act of violence or not can be determined, not by reference to the grounds on which it affects the party against whom it is directed. Thus both act of violence and act of non-violence may have a just or an unjust cause. So no one can claim to be absolutely in right. Pursuit of truth, therefore, doesnot admit of violence being inflicted on one's opponent who must be weaned from error by patience and sympathy by self-suffering. It also attacks not only the sin and the evil, but also the sinner and evil doer. It is offending against the great truth, unity and sacredness of all being.[66] Pursuit of truth means realisation of the unity of the great truth through love and service of all. But in practical we find that violence interferes with this realization of such unity.

Non-violence thus is the practical application of the great truth of Spiritual unity, the spiritual democracy of all life. The basic principle on which the practice of non-violence rests is that what holds good in respect of oneself equally applies to the whole universe. It is the heart of all religion, the means and the end, and so it is truth itself, its very soul,. its maturest fruit.[67] The jewel of ahimsa was discovered during the search for and contemplation of truth.[68] Gandhi's experience convinced him that if one let go his hold of truth, he would never be able to solve the riddle of ahimsa.[69] For him truth is the highest law and ahimsa is the highest duty.[70] Like truth ahimsa is also omnipotent, infinite and synonymous with God, the soul force, the power of the Godhead within each and every finite being. As the soul can exist independently of the physical body, in the same way ahimsa also transcends time and space, and act independently of physical aids. It is the greatest and the most active force in the world, more positive than electricity, more powerful than each other superior to all the forces put together, the only force in life.

We believe that non-violence is infinitely superior to violence, forgiveness is more manly than punishment, Abstinence is forgiveness only when there is the power to punish; it is meaningless when it pretends to proceed from a helpless creature. A mouse hardly forgives a cat when it allows itself to be torn to pieces.[71] Non-violence is in fact law of our species, as violence is the law of brute, because the spirit is dormant in the brute, and he knows no law except the law of physical might. But the dignity of man needs acceptance of higher law to the strength of spirit. The *Rishis,* who discovered the law of non-violence in the midst of violence, were greater geniuses than Newton; greater warriors than Wellington. Inspite of knowledge of the use of arms, they realized their uselessness, and taught a weary world that its salvation lay not through violence but through non-violence.

Non-violence in its dynamic condition means conscious suffering. It does not mean submission to the will of the evil doer, but it means putting of one's whole soul against the will of the evil doer. Being a potent force, non-violence begins with mind. Non-violence of the mere body without the cooperation of the mind is non-violence of the weak without any potency. It is infact not in any shape or form of a passive or inactive method, but essentially an active movement, much active than the use of sanguinary weapons. It resides in the human breast and actively works their way, whether one is sleeping or not, walking lisurely or playing an active game. The panopiled warrior of truth and non-violence is ever and incessantly active. Non-violence is like radium in its action. An infinitesimal quantity of it embeded in a malignant growth, acts continuously, silently and ceaselessly till it has transformed the whole mass of the diseased tissue into a healthy one. In the same way even a little of true non-violence acts in a silent, subtle, unseen way and leavens the whole society.

Like truth, non-violence is also a matter of faith and experience, a quality of the hearts and souls, and not a mental or intellectual attitude.[72] Like Plato, Gandhi also advocated that the universe is governed by non-violence and love, for life persists in the midst of destruction, but man doesnot live by destruction. Man lives by attraction and self love which compels regard for others.[73] Because where there is love, there is life, and hatred leads to destruction.[74] Non-violence is thus an all pervasive eternal principle applicable to every walk of life without any exception. This is the cause of Gandhi's insistence that when non-violence is accepted as the law of life, it pervades the whole being and not applied to isolated acts, as a condition of complete success of non-violence.[75] He also believes like Tolstoy that once we admit violence into non-violence, we admit the insufficiency of the latter and deny it as the law of moral life. It is the kingdom of heaven and if one seeks it first, everything else shall be added unto us. Non-violence is thus only the thing that matters. It is at the root of each and every one's activities and is placed before while it is professed, and then alone it becomes irresistable.[76]

Non-violence or ahimsa is seemingly negative in its form because of its negative prefixes 'A' and 'Non', Gandhi said that *hinsa* is an inherent necessity for life in the body. So ahimsa means an effort to abondon the violence that is inevitable in life.[77] Ahimsa stands for the ultimate deliverence of man from the bondage of the flesh, so that one can attain the state in which life is possible without the necessity of a perishable body whose sustenance inevitably involves destruction. The negative aspect of ahimsa consists in refraining from causing pain or killing any life out of anger of for selfish interests. It thus consists avoiding of injury to anything, living being, upon this earth in thought, word and deed.

Ahimsa does not simply mean non-killing refraining from causing pain or killing any life out of anger, but Gandhi points out the insidious forms of hinsa, harsh words and judgements, ill will, anger, torture, cruelty, starvation, humiliation and oppression of the weak, killing of theirself respect.[78] R. B. Gragg defines violence, that it is any act, motive, thought, active feeling or outwardly directed attitude which is divisive in nature or result that is called inconsistant with spiritual unity. It includes pride, scorn contempt, anger, gambling, spite, indignation, and killing, wounding, exploiting, deceiving flattering etc.[79] Thus ahimsa in the negative sense requires that one may not harbour an uncharitable thought, even in connection with one who may consider himself our enemy. To him the test of hinsa is a violent intention behind a thought, word or deed; an intention to harm.

Killing is thus not hinsa when life is destroyed for the sake of those whose life is taken. The destruction of such life who's body are tortured and suffering the pangs of slow, certain death, is called ahimsa. Gandhi laid some conditions which warrants the taking of life of an ailing individual from the point of view of ahimsa, for its fulfilment.

(i) The disease should be incurable.
(ii) All corcerned should have despaired of the life of the patient.
(iii) The case should be beyond all help or service.
(iv) It should be impossible for the patient in question to express his or its wish.[80]

Gandhi advocated that if my child be attacked by rabies and there is no helpful remedy to relieve his agony, I would consider it my duty to take his life.[81] Forcibly preventing a child from rushing towards fire and smacking a child from biting by a snake to keep it awake are non-violence, only provided that the motive must not be anger but the desire to save child from injury.[82] Thus ahimsa is mistaken for a purely negative doctrine. For Gandhi it is essentially a positive and dynamic force. In its positive and active form means love and benevolence in much comprehensive than the pauline sense because it includes the whole creation and not merely human being. It also includes sub-human life, including plants and animals. It is in its real sense of the term an active form of goodwill towards all life upon this universe.

Simply refraining from violence is the real non-violence, and love is its very soul. But Gandhi does not identify non-violence with love in order to distinguish the spiritual force of non-violence from the grosser aspect of the connotation of love. Non-violence, that is love, is not necessary affair based upon the goodness of the object of love. But true love is such that is self-effacing and demands no consideration.[83] True love consists in transferring itself from the body to the dweller within, and then necessarily realising the oneness of all life inhabiting countless bodies.[84] The real love is to love them who hate love and a man to whom no one trusts. All living things including plants and animals have kinship with human beings, being God's creation like mankind, possess right to live. One and all habit of killing fellow beings on the slightest pretext has darkened one's reason. One has no right to destroy life that one cannot create. The fullest development of man needs the largest love that sheds all fear and reaches out to all creatures.[85]

Non-violence in its deepest sense of the term holds the greatest love, love for good and evil doer. It doesnot mean mere surrender to the will of the opponent the evil one, but putting of one's whole soul against the will of the tyrant, because evil cannot be controlled by evil or violence. To apply violence against the evil doer is to deny spiritual unity within him. To repeat the act done by evil doer, to repeat the mistake of the evil doer, to fight against evil with the weapon of the evil-doer (violence) is same taking out by satan, to step down to the level of the evil doer, to cooperate and collaborate with him in propogating evil. This means simply to move around in a vicious circle.

Non-violence seeks to conquer evil by good. It stands for moral opposition to immortality the resistance of soul against physical force. It goes to the very root of the problem, believes in the ultimate possibility, the goodness of human nature and refuses to accept the evil doer at his own valuation. It by conscious suffering and love force tries to convert the evil doer to make one conscious of spiritual kingship with the victim. In fact love does not burn others, but it burns itself. It implies that the ahimsaist achieves the complete self purification as far as in humanly possible, and develops internal strength by a victorious conflict against one's own feeling of resentment, which on the other hand comes out in form of retaliation and hatred. A man of non-violence, conquers his own self and tries to arouse in the heart of the evil doer a sense of love and justice. Non-violence consists is allowing others the maximum of convenience at the maximum of inconvenience. Every act of injury to a living being and endorsement of such act by refraining from non-violent effort to prevent it, is in fact a breach of non-violence.[86] Non-violence in its highest form, in its absolute form is called absolute ahimsa, which means perfect freedom from violence (ahimsa) and overflowing, understanding love for all. This state of complete non-violence, the stage when all violence, whatever form are eschewed, is in fact a perfect state of non-violence. It is attained only when mind, body and speech are in perfect coordination. It is in itself a power the absolute power the real attribute of God.

But inspite of being a strong advocator of non-violence Gandhi passed his opinion the underlying ahimsa is the unity of all life, the error of one cannot affect one but one and all, and hence man cannot be wholly free from violence. So long as one continues to be social being, he cannot but participate in the violence that the very existence of society involves.[87] Life is bound in a chain of destruction and violence is an inherent necessity for life, so no one in flesh and blood could remain completely free from violence.[88] Man has to destroy some life not only for sustaining one's own body, but also for protecting those under one's care. The very fact of one's living, eating, drinking and movement involves some destruction of life. This is why Gandhi advocated that these are inevitable hinsa and so these are permissible. Here Gandhi differs from Mahavira. Apart from hinsa in eating, drinking etc, he gave several instances where one cannot avoid hinsa killing tigres and snakes; in emergency destroying infectious rats and fleas etc; killing a murderer who is about to kill other person if he cannot be prevented by some other means. These all instances and all such instances, where (violence) hinsa is unavoidable are called 'Duty in distress', which comes out from human imperfections. But these doesnot disprove the validity of ahimsa which is the supreme value and law of life. The greater one progresses towards perfection, one gets knowledge of non-violent ways of dealing with exceptional duties and less the need to fall back on violent expedients. The votary of non-violence is to remain true to one's faith, the inevitable hinsa (violence) must be spontaneous, though not thoughtless, must be the lowest and minimum, rooted in compassion and have discriminations, restraint and detachment at its back.[89] It is committed when all remedies to avoid it are exhausted.[90]

Causing pain or killing may be —

(i) Non-violence, when it is the result of calm and clear judgement, and the intention is to benefit the victim and his or her agony rather than to relieve the pain caused to the ahinsaist by his agony;
(ii) Violence is permissible when it is restored to for sustaining one's body or protecting one's wards; and
(iii) Violence, when life is taken out of anger selfishness or ill-will.

To decide finally that whether a particular act or abstention can be classed as non-violence, a reference to both deed and intent is essential. But to kill or give injury to any living being to save one's own interest is violence or hinsa, however noble the motive may otherwise be. A man who harbours illwill towards others is also guilty of hinsa, because for fear of society or in want of opportunity, he is unable to act according to this ill-will.

Non-violence thus rules out all want on violence to the sub-human creation. It is not a mere matter of dietetics, but it transcends it. What a man eats or drinks matters little. It is the self denial, self restraint behind it that matters.[91] Non-violence implies that one must engage in occupations that involve the least violence; fundamentally free from violence and involves no exploitation of others. Freer a man becomes from violence, nearer he comes to perfect non-violence to Absolute, Truth or God.

Going to a far extent in the principles of non-violence, Gandhi advocated that there are three levels of non-violence. The first and the foremost one is called "The enlightened non-violence of resourcefulness or the non-violence of the brave". It is the non-violence of one who adopts it not by painful necessity but by inner conviction based on moral considerations. Such kind of non-violence pervades each and every sphere of life. It is non-violence which never calculates and bends. One adopts non-violence as the law of life not because it serves the purpose, but because one reaches that state of moral progress at which violence is intolerable. At such a state non-violence moves mountains, transforms life and flinches from nothing in its unshakable faith. The people who accept non-violence as a creed never surrender's

because it is the law of out species.[98] Working under the law of non-violence, it is possible for a single individual to defy the whole might to save honour, religion, soul, and lies the foundation of regeneration. It is soul force or the power of Godhead within human being.

Non-violence thus a creed all pervasive, law of out species has of itself five axioms as pleaded by the Gandhi.

(i) Non-violence implies a complete self purification as is humanly possible;
(ii) Man for man, the strength of non-violence is in exact proportion to the ability, not the will, of the non-violent person to inflict violence;
(iii) Non-violence is without exception superior to violence;
(iv) There is no such thing as defeat in non-violence. The end of violence is surest defeat; and
(v) The ultimate end of non-violence is surest victory if such a term may be used of non-violence. In reality where there is no sense of defeat, there is no sense of victory.[99]

Non-violence is not a cloistered virtue but applicable in the forum and the legislatures as in the market place.[100] It depends upon certain pre-conditions for the implication and practice of non-violence for its success. Those certain pre-conditions are :

(i) Non-violence is the law of the human race and is infinitely greater than and superior to brute force;
(ii) Consciousness of the living presence of God within one is the foremost requisite. It does not avail to those who donot possess a living faith in God or Love;
(iii) Non-violence demands on the part of its practitioner perfect humality;
(iv) It demands purity of heart, courage, forgiveness, and fearlessness;
(v) It demands complete abstention from exploitation and non-possession;
(vi) Non-violence, in the very nature of things, is of no assistance in the defence of ill goten gains and immoral acts; and
(vii) Non-violence, a power wielded by all children, young men and women or grown up people, provided they have love and faith in God and equal love for all mankind. Non-violence as a law of life pervades the whole being and not be applied to

isolated acts.

Thus philosophy of non-violence is meant for the common people and the salvation of mankind lies only through non-violence. The doctrine constitutes the core of Jainism and Buddhism. But the Gandhi's distinction and unique contribution lies in the fact that he gave to non-violence, an extended meaning and application. The points which draw our attention are that the main spring of non-violence is love, and its true criterion is the inner feeling in the human heart. It is wrong to think that since one cannot observe complete non-violence, one should not try to observe the little one can finally that the more one practice love and compassion, the more one increase them, and becomes morally elevated and truely happy.[101]

Fearlessness

Fearlessness, the another ethical principle, the discipline of Satyagraha, is indispensable for the development of truth and non-violence. Fear lies at the root of untruth and violence, and so cowardice is the outcome of fear. Cowardice in itself is possibly the greatest violence, far greater than bloodshed and the like that go under the name of violence. It comes from want of faith in God and ignorance of attributes of God. Truth and non-violence can be cultivated only by the strong and strength lies in absence of fear and not in the quantity of flesh and blood, we have on our bodies.[102] Gandhi lays a great stress upon fearlessness, considering it the sign of self-purification and defines *Swaraj* as the abandonment of fear of death.[103] Fearlessness is essential for the growth of the other noble qualities. Pritam says, the path of Hari is the path of the brave, not of cowards. Hari means truth and the brave are those armed with fearlessness.[104] Viscount Samuel remarks that Mahatma Gandhi taught the Indian to straighten their back, to raise their eyes, and to face circumstances with steady gaze.[105]

Fearlessness connotes freedom from all external fear; fear of disease, bodily injury and death, of dispossession, of losing one's near and dear one, of losing reputation or giving offences and so on. Gandhi said that one and all must fear God and cease to fear man. All the fears revolve round the body as the centre and would, therefore, disappear as soon as one gets rid of attachment for the body.[106] To develop non-attachment one and all must conquer one's own possions, the internal foes. It requires a balance state of mind or mental equipoise by means of control of passions, which is termed, the Gita,

'Shitaprajana'. This is the state in which man conquers himself and also external fears cease of their own accord. This state is possible to one who has had a glimpse of treatment that transcends the body. Such an individual acquires the capacity to make sacrifice of the highest form. Those who sets his head upon death as his pillow, are great ones. They defy death and are free from all fear and becomes fearless.[107] Also need of prayer and of unflinching obedience to dictates of conscience, for the voice of conscience is the will of God and final judge of the rightness of every need and thought for fearlessness.[108] Determined and constant endeavour, and cultivation of self-confidence are also necessary for fearlessness.

The principle of abhaya or fearlessness is also found in ancient writings, and the Mahatma derived it from love and regarded fearlessness, a necessary quality for a spiritual life, specially for practise of truth and non-violence. He adopted it as the pre-conditional quality for the practise of non-violence and also essential for the growth of the other noble qualities. One cannot seek truth or cherish love without fearlessness.[109] Moral bravery is in fact the greatest heroism, and it consists not in striking or injuring others, but in the readiness to sacrifice patiently and fearlessly everything including life for the good of other fellow beings, out of love for all of them. Fearlessness is in fact the essential precondition to practise non-violence and to insistence on truth. In absence of this very quality one can never become a true Satyagrahi.

Swadeshi

Of all the vows advocated by Mahatma Gandhi Swadeshi is an important one. It stands for its English counterpart 'Indegenous' meaning a thing manufactured in one's own country. It is, in fact, a religious discipline to be undergone in utter disregard of the physical discomfort. It may cause to the individual, which is called sacred law of our being. The principle of Swadeshi is engrained in the basis nature of man.

The inherent nature and object of *Swadeshi* is in no way political but spiritual. It has power to enable an individual to realise the spiritual unity of it through out the life, Swadeshi, in its ultimate and spiritual sense, stands for the last and final release of the soul from this earthly bondage, because body is a hinderence to the fullest realization of this spritual unity and is not the natural or permanent abode of the soul.[110] In absence of such realization, one cannot attain such kind of spiritual unity by going through the service of God's creation and proper way of such kind of service lies in the *Swadeshi*. *Swadeshi* is in fact a law, which lays down the only correct method of serving God's creation. The law in that spiritt is one and all human beings which resists us the use and service of our immediate surroundings to the exclusion of the more remote.[111] It is that kind of spirit which dictated man to serve one's next door neighbour to the exclusion of any other. The condition is that the neighbour thus served had in his turn to serve his own neighbour.

Swadeshi in its root is an multidymensional and all sided patriotism of an exelted spiritual kind. It implies that one and all must serve the country of birth in perference to others. To serve the country one must serve the immediate neighbourhood in perference to remote places inside the country. It also demands that one must hold fast to countries ideals and institutions. But this does not mean a blind, unthinking attachment to the familiar institutions, but a discrimination regard for them with a readiness to reform and borrow from others whatever is really healthy and fruitful.

The essence and inherent quality of Swadeshi is the purity of service. It never seeks for some, neglecting the all. It never countenances and promotes the advancement of illegitimate, narrow selfish interests of few neglecting the interest of the which and also of humanity.It only requires from one to discharge one's legitimate obligation to one's neighbour's, and to prepare them to sacrifice themselves, at the altar of humanity and universal services. The spirit of sacrifice, which underlines Swadeshi, goes beyond man's community and embraces the whole of humanity. The logical conclusion of self sacrifice is that the individual sacrifices himself for the community, the community sacrifices itself for the district, district sacrifices for the province, the province sacrifices for the nation and the nation for the world.[112] One can serve his nighbours and humanity at the same time. But the condition is that the service of the neighbour is in no way exclusive or selfish. It doesnot involve the exploitation of any other human being. Everyone would understand the very spirit in which such service is given. They would also know that they would give the others. The spirit of self sacrifice implies that a truely free country is bound to run with the help of his neighbours. This is why Gandhi beautifully termed Swadeshi as the acme of universal service,[113] which implies performance of the nearest and the immediate. It is because man's knowledge of the world in which one lives remains limited. So one has his first duty to dedicate themselves to the service of the immediate neighbours the nearest and the best known. Besides this, if one serves people of distant places one is guilty of two offences, guilty of culpable neglect of his neighbours who have claim on his service. His attempt would be also an unintended disservice to the people of the distant places, for he disturbs the atmosphere of the new place in his ignorance. Also it is an arrogance to think of serving distant places when one is hardly able to serve even his neighbours.[114] It recognizes the scientific limitation of human capability for service.[115] It is better to die performing one's duty or swadharma, but *paradharma* or others duty is fraught with danger. This applies to Swadeshi, for Swadeshi is always applied to one's immediate environment.

Swadeshi in itself consists and permeates the whole philosophy of Gandhi, his views on culture, metaphysical and ethical ideas, social and political theory, views on education and his economic outlook. The view of culture as snapped by the Mahatma, the concept of *Swadeshi* finds in its full expression, in his maticulous attachment to the rural civilization of the country due to its spiritual and non-violent values and their perception. Gandhi was not an indiscriminate despiser of everything western, but he condemns in no uncertain terms the materialism and violence of modern civilization; a race after power and pleasure, it neglects the soul and its perfection. For the Mahatma, modern civilization is ephemeral and a civilization only in name.[116]

The metaphysical and ethical ideas of Gandhi, are firmly rooted in the philosophical tradition of the country. He interpreted ancient ideals and applied them to modern life. The principle of *Swadeshi* consists the idea and thought of religion as advocated by Gandhi. As for religion, I must restrict myself to any ancestral religion that is the use of immediate religious surroundings. If I find it defective I should serve it by purging it of its defects,[117] said the Mahatma. Also in the sociopolitical spheres he told that Swadeshi plays an important role in making use of indigenous institutions and curing them of their proved defects. All the non-violent methods in fact are the refined and modernized forms of ancient Indian modes of political and social protest. In social field, he upholded the *Varnashramadharma.*

But apart from all above mentioned facts,the most important of all regarding *Swadeshi* as advocated by Gandhi is the economic thought. He strongly argued for the self sufficiency of the people, even of people living in villages, except for such foreign things as are needed for the growth of the people.[118] The broad definition of Swadeshi is the use of all home made articles to the exclusion of foreign things, in so far as such use is necessary for the protection of home industries, more specially those industries without which India will panperised. The view of Swadeshi have undergone in a course of evolution in thoughts of Gandhi. His thoughts reveals that he stood for complete self sufficiency of the country and its economic isolation from the rest of the world. He said, if not an article of commerce had been brought from outside India, she would be a land of milk and honey. We can live for ourselves if we would produce our all requirements within our own limitations and border.[119]

Swadeshi in its totality demands the exclusion of all foreign goods. Gandhi introduced Khadi as the symbol of Swadeshi, decentralized economy, a universal subsidiary industry on which the semi-starved and semi-employed people can depend to take out their scanty income. This is why Gandhi considered *Khadi* as a necessary and the most important corollary of the principle of Swadeshi. It is the first indispensable step towards the discharge of Swadeshi dharma towards society. But the economic aspect of Swadeshi dharma does not end with Khadi. It implies a comprehensive preference of local goods and boycott of all foreign cloth and articles which can be produced in one's own country, through not all foreign goods. Gandhi observed that the centre of Swadeshi lies in Khadi. If Khadi goes, there is no Swadeshi because the Indian people with the mill productions do not constitute Swadeshi.[120] The economic aspect of Swadeshi begins with Khadi and it implies in itself a comprehensive preference of local production and boycott of everything that is not of our own Country.

But Gandhi brilliantly made a clear distinction between the economic aspect of Swadeshi and the economic boycott of foreign goods. Swadeshi infact is a spiritual discipline, an invigorating and purifying process, and a constructive programme. He conceded the economic boycott of foreign articles as a temporary punitive measure, a weapon of expediency, which works as undue influence exerted to secure one's purpose. It is infact to compel the others by deliberately inflicting a loss on them and the spirit of punishment is a sign of weakness and a form of violence. But these economic boycott doesnot need to be vindictive and violent. It should be used as a legitimate non-violent and non-coercive means of non-cooperation.[121]

Inspite of all virtues, mentioned earlier, without humility all goes in vain for humility is essential for a non-violent individual seeker after truth. The complete annihilation of the body is possible only by reason and complete annihilation of the body is Salvation. Complete destruction of ego results in an embodiment of truth. It is a sense of moral and spiritual proportion whereby all individual souls are related to the infinite and eternal God and than assume their true place and position. True humility means most strenuous and constant endeavour, entirely directed to the service of humanity.[122] This kind of humility has also a pre-condition, named self purification. In other sense humility is also a kind of self purification, which involves the constant cultivation of all above mentioned cardinal virtues or discipline. These all ethical and metaphysical discipline involves the control and sublimation of divisive appetites and emotions, particularly those of sex, acquisitive-ness, pugnacity, fear and hatred. The discipline is in fact a singular blending of different inward acts of conscience which issue in outward acts of observance.[123] Gandhi insists on mind, body and speech, in proper coordination, for the mere outward observance will be simply a mask harmful both to man himself and others.[124] The various observances being derived from truth are inter-related, and we cannot regard any of them without hurting the rest, because all the disciplines are of equal importance. If one is broken all are broken. So it requires that essentially all the disciplines should be taken with equal importance as one.

Gandhi accepted the traditional virtues, but the great work he did is that he refashioned all those virtues in keeping with the temper of the age and demand of the time and situation. These all disciplines are eternal laws of life preached for thousand of years. But these ideals lacked the vitality, fullness of meaning and universality of application which they possess today. They had been regarded as cloistered virtues, the exclusive preserve of the ascetic or a mere mask for the weak and the coward. They were conceded as correct ideas, but dismissed for being not practical in the different sphere of life.

Truth has no place in trade and commerce, in professions like law and politics. Even after the ministers of Buddha and Christ, non-violence has not been regarded as an adequate method of resolving all kinds of conflicts, and of organizing society, regulating individual and group relations. Its use is confined to isolated individuals and small groups. He restated and reinterpreted all these fundamental laws in terms of modern life. He experimented with all disciplines on a larger sphere than anyone else had and applied them in original way to each and every aspect of life practically. For its practical utility, he created suitable organizations and got trained all his followers. He preached and demonstrated that all these disciplines or ideals are for whole humanity and can be practised in every walk of life. He also proved to a sceptical world that truth and non-violence are the mightiest weapon in the hands of we people, the inexhaustible source of power and energy. Gandhi, to his par-excellence enriched the content of all the disciplines, and gave a new life into them.

But how far all these discipline are relevant and practicable is a question to be discussed. It is so because Gandhi has expected too much of human nature. How far all these ideals really lead to the greatest good of all either metaphysical or ethical. On the other hand if we for a moment accept all the ideals fully sound and fruitful, problems does not left our way. Here we find that there in whole thought of Gandhi we do not find the way how to apply all these abstract principles to concrete situations of life. In this work I propose to deal with all these dificulties in forthcoming chapters.

REFERENCES

1. Paul, F. Power, *Gandhi on World Affairs,* George Allen & Unwin Ltd., London, 1961, p. 35
2. Gandhi, M. K., *Young India,* April 14, 1927, p. 120.
3. Raju, P. T., *Idealistic Thought of India,* Chap. VII, pp. 292-93.
4. Gandhi, M.K., *Young India,* October 23, 1924, p. 350.
5. Gandhi, M.K., *Harijan,* December 24, 1938, p. 393.
6. Ghosal, U.N., *A History of Hindu Political Theories,* Oxford Univ. Press, London, 1927, p. 11 quoted in The *Evolution of Political Philosophy* of M. Gandhi, B. D. Bhattacharya, p. 70.
7. Albert Schweitzer, *Indian Thought and Its Development,* Tr. Mrs. Charles, E. B. Russell, Adam and Charles Black, London, 1956, p. 235.
8. Roy, B. Gopal, *Gandhian Ethics,* Navjivan Pub., 1950, pp. 3-4.

9 & 10. Louis Fischer, *The Life of Mahatma Gandhi,* Bhartiya Vidya Bhawan, Bombay, 1955, Part-I, p. 25.

11. *Non-Violance in Politics; A Study of Gandhian Techniques and Thinking,* Frank Bros & Co., Delhi, 1958, p. 133-134.
12. Gandhi, M.K., *Harijan* , February 10, 1940, p. 445.
13. Ayer & Ganesan, *Ethical Relision,* p. 23-24.
14. Gandhi, M.K., *Harijan,* May 14, 1938, p. 109.
15. Gandhi, M.K., *Harijan,* June 03/1939, p. 146.
16. Gandhi, M.K., *Harijan.* July 20, 1947, p. 240.
17. Gandhi, M.K., *Harijan,* October 13, 1940, p. 318.
18. Gandhi, M.K., *Harijan,* August 18, 1940, p. 256.
19. Gandhi, M.K., *Harijan,* October 13, 1940, pp. 318-19.
20. Gandhi, M.K., *Young India,* March 1925, p. 80-81.
21. Gandhi, M.K., *Yeravada Mandir,* p.1.
22. Gandhi, M.K., *Harijan,* November 14, 1936, p. 314.
23. Radhakrishnan, S. & J. Muirhead, *Contemporary Indian Philosophy,* London, 1958, p. 21.
24. Gandhi, M.K., *Young India,* March 5, 1925, p. 81.
25. Datta, D. M., *The Philosophy of Mahatma Gandhi,* 1953, p. 26.
26. Datta D.M., *The Philosophy of Mahatma Gandhi,* 1953, p. 06.
27. Datta, D.M., *The Philosophy of Mahatma Gandhi,* 1953, pp. 30-31.
28. Roy, Binoy Gopal, *Gandhian Ethics,* Navjivan, 1950, pp. 3-4.

29. Gandhi, M.K., *Harijan* , May 6, 1933, p. 120.
30. Gandhi, M.K., *Harijan* June 3, 1939, p. 151.
31. Gandhi, M.K., *Harijan,* June 13, 1930, p. 163.
32. Gandhi, M.K., *Harijan,* December 26, 1936, p. 365.
33. Tendulker, D.G., *Life of Mahatma Gandhi,* 1961, Vol. II, p. 189.
34. Radhakrishnan S., & Muirhead, *Contemparary Indian Philosophy,* 1958, p. 21.
35. Raju, P. T., *Idealistic Thought of India,* London, 1953 Chapter VII, p. 297.
36. Datta, D. M., *Philosophy of Mahatma Gandhi,* 1953, p. 40.
37. John, V. Bondurant, *Conquest of Violance: The Gandhian Philosophy of Conflict* Oxford Univ. Press, 1959, p. 193.
38. Bose, N.K., *Studies in Gandhism,* 1947, p. 269.
39. Datta, D.M., *The Philosophy of Mahatma Gandhi,* 1953, p. 42.
40. Datta, D.M., *The Pholosophy of Mahatma Gandhi,* 1953, p. 44.
41 & 42. Gandhi, M.K., *Ethical Religion,* Tr. A. Ramaiyer & S. Ganesan, Madras, 1922, p. 19.
43. Gandhi, M.K., *Ethical Religion,* p. 15.
44. Gandhi, M.K., *Ethical Religion,* p. 279.
45. Gandhi, M.K., *Young India,* July 21, 1920, p. 4.
46. Osborn, *R., Humanism & Moral Theory,* London, 1959, p. 93.
47. Gandhi, M.K., *Ethical Religion,* p. 6.
48. Gandhi, M.K., *Ethical Religion,* p. 7.
49. Gandhi, M.K., *Ethical Religion,* Tr. by A. Ramaiyar & S. Ganesan, 1922, Madras.
50. Gandhi, M. K., *Yeravada Mandir,* p. 02.
51. Gandhi, M.K., *Harijan,* May 25, 1935, p. 115.
52. Gandhi, M.K., *Young India,* September 17, 1925. (Satyam bruyat, Priyam Bruyat, Na Bruyat Satyam Apriyam).
53. Gandhi, M.K., *Satyagraha in South Africa,* p. 433.
54. Gandhi, M.K., *Harijan,* May 25, 1935, p. 114.
55. Gandhi, M.K., *Harijan,* November 27, 1449, p. 340.
56. Gandhi, M.K., *Young India,* II, p. 1182.
57. Gandhi, M.K., *Harijan,* Feburary 6, 1937, p. 414.
58. Radhakrishanan , S. , *Mahatma Gandhi,* p. 80-81.
59. Gandhi, M.K., *Yeravada Mandir,* p. 16.
60. Spratt, P., *Gandhism: An Analysis,* The Huxley Press, Madras, 1939, p. 146-47.
61. Bose, N. K., *My Days With Gandhi,* pp. 55-56.
62. Gandhi, M.K., *Autobiography,* p. 427.
63. Gandhi, M.K., *Young India,* August 25, 1920, p. 02.
64. Desai, Mahadeo, *Autobiography,* Gandhi, M.K., p. 427.
65. Gandhi, M.K., *Yeravada Mandir,* p. 8-9 & 14.
66. Gandhi, M.K., *Autobiography,* II, p. 53-54.
67. Gandhi, M.K., *Young India,* II, 936 & III, p. 154.
68. Kripalini, J.B., *The Gandhian Way,* Bombay, 1938.
69. Gandhi, M.K., *Autobiography,* II, p. 476.
70. Gandhi, M.K., *Harijan,* March 28, 1936, p. 49.
71. Gandhi, M.K., *Young India,* August 11, 1920, p. 03. .
72. Gandhi, M.K., *Young India,* II, p. 1113.
73. Gandhi, M. K., *Young India,* I, p. 284.
74. Gandhi, M.K., *Young India,* I, p. 734.
75. Gandhi, M.K.,*Harijan,* September 5, 1936, p. 237.
76. Gandhi, M.K., *Harijan,* June 24, 1939, p. 174.

77. Gandhi, M.K., *Harijan,* September 1, 1940, p. 271.
78. Gandhi, M.K., *Young India,* III, p. 860.
79. Gregg, R.B., *The Power of Non-violance,* Ahmedabad, 1938, p. 282.
80. Gandhi, M.K.,*Young India,* III, p. 897.
81. Gandhi, M.K.,*Young India,* II, p. 978.
82. Gandhi, M. K., *Hind Swaraj,* 1958, pp. 65-66.
83. Gandhi, M.K.,*Young India,* II,p. 551.
84. Gandhi, M.K., *Bapu's Letters to Mira,* Ahmedabad, 1949, p. 157.
85. Gandhi, M.K., *Harijan,* January 9, 1937, p. 382.
86. Gandhi, M.K.,*Young India,* III, p. 812.
87. Gandhi, M.K., *Autobiography,* II, p. 229.
88. Gandhi, M.K., *Autobiography,* II, p. 229.
89 & 90. Gandhi M.K., *Young India,* II, p. 971-83.
91. Gandhi, M.K., *Young India* ,III, p. 821.
92. Gandhi, M.K.,*Young India,* March 26, 1931, p. 49.
93. Gandhi, M.K., *Harijan,* July 27, 1947, p. 253.
94. Gandhi, M.K., *Hind Swaraj,* Ahmedabad, 1958, p. 40.
95. Gandhi, M.K., *Harijan* ,October 21, 1939, p. 310.
96. Gandhi, M.K., *Hind Swaraj,* Ahmedabad, 1958, pp. 68-69.
97. Gandhi, M.K., *Young India,* December 21, 1931.
98. Gandhi, M.K., *Harijan,* November 4, 1939, p. 331.
99. Gandhi, M.K., *Harijan,* October 12, 1935, p. 276.
100. Gandhi, M.K., *Harijan,* May 8, 1937, p. 98.
101. Datta, D.M., *The Philosophy of Mahatma Gandhi,* p. 100.
102. Gandhi, M.K., *Hind Swaraj,* 1958, p. 29.
103. Gandhi, M.K., *Young India,* I, p. 898.
104. Gandhi, M.K., *Yeravada Mandir,* March 6, 1932, p. 27.
105. Radhakrishnan, S., *Mahatma Gandhi: Essays and reklections of his Life and Work,* London, 1939, p. 295.
106. Gandhi, M.K., *Yeravada Mandir,* p. 45.
107. Gandhi, M.K., *Hind Swaraj,* p. 73.
108. Gandhi, M.K., *Ethical Religion,* p. 41.
109. Gandhi, M.K., *Yeravada Mandir,* p. 27.
110. Gandhi, M.K., *Yeravada Mandir,* p. 89.
111. Natesen, G. A., *Speeches and Writings of Mahatma Gandhi,* Madras,1922, p. 27.
112. Natesen, G,A., *Speeches and Writings of Mahatma Gandhi,* p. 281.
113. Gandhi, M.K., *Yeravada Mandir,* p. 93.
114. Natesen, G.A., *Speeches and writings of Mahatma Gandhi,* p. 281.
115. Gandhi, M.K., *Harijan,* March 23, 1947, p. 79.
116. Gandhi, M.K., *Hind Swaraj,* Chapters VI & XIII.
117. Natesen, G.A., *Speeches and Writings of Mahatma Gandhi,* p. 278.
118. Natesen, G.A., *Speeches and Writings of Mahatma Gandhi,* p. 27.
119. Natesen, G.A., *Speeches and Writings of Mahatma Gandhi,* p. 27.
120. Gandhi, M.K., *Harijan,* June 29, 1947, p. 211.
121. Gandhi, M.K., *Hind Swaraj,* Chapter IX.
122. Gandhi, M.K., *Yeravada Mandir,* p. 69.
123. Andrews, C.F., *Mahatma Gandhi's Ideas,* Allen and Anwin, London, 1929, p. 111.
124. Gandhi, M.K., *Young India,* October 1, 1931, p. 287.

5

CONTRADICTIONS IN DIFFERENT FORMS OF SATYAGRAHA

The present chapter enumerates the contradictions inherent in forms of Satyagraha i.e. non-cooperation, Civil Disobedience etc. as depicted by Gandhi.

Non-cooperation and Civil Disobedience

Gandhi's theories of non-cooperation and civil disobedience establish a new principle of non-violence. According to Gandhi, non-cooperation should be completely non-violent. But some other thinkers presume that it may or may not be violent in practice. In the context of Gandhi's view on non-cooperation, it itself proves a violent-like means. The incident occurred at Chauri-Chaura is an ample example of practical invalidity in Gandhian conception of non-violence. In fact, being an idealist thinker Gandhi emphasies on pure idea rather than its practical implication. This drawback presents in his all the arguments. It seems that all his arguments have a basis that ideas quo ideas, if restricted to the region of ideas, possess no dynamic force. He has mistaken in realising that ideas are winged words that carry disaster and death. Ideas are active by themselves and being an idea prior to action, non-cooperation is always as active as a mere idea. It is as active as a mere idea when translated into action. But whenever any idea becomes active in human mind, it necessarily conflicts with some other ideas, and in such a state idea becomes violent when it meets another activity. Non-cooperation is also necessarily violent because being an idea first it comes in conflict with other ideas opposed to it. To keep non-cooperation in the domain of ideas does not confer upon it any immunity from violence. The spirit of violence, if not acts of violence, is the basic content in the idea of non-cooperation. Gandhi is not logical in theory and practice of non-cooperation based upon reason. He ignored the basic physiological character of human being, the existence of idea in human brain. The another problem related to non-cooperation is what extent it can be applied in practice by a human being. An individual can independently practice non-cooperation non-violently in full swing, but it is not necessarily always true that a group of human being will collectively be non-violent too in the application of non-cooperation. For instance being a responsible men A, B and C all three should be peaceful, gentle and moral. But in their own behaviour or action they prove themselves very different. Their actions are different not only in quantity but also in quality. A man always acts for himself as well as for society.

In other words, there are two kinds of human actions individual and social. By individual action a man satisfies his own needs. But he has a duty to satisfy his own family's needs as well as to fulfil the task of his own social welfare. Thus a man's action is also collective in nature, in regard to social welfare. In fact man in society, in their collective form is not the same as man as an individual. One's social behaviour is often different from his behaviour as an individual. For instance an Indian, courteous and quiet mannered in his individual life, acts or may act like a dancing devishes on the floor of the parliament. The truth which underlies the human psychology is that the social atmosphere of the creed losses the moral fibre of even its basic ethical axioms. History is evidence that crowd in never found intellect in any age. It is a part of individual. In our practical life in compare to action of an individual which might be peaceful action of a crowd remains under an iron discipline for a certain period of time, under a great stress, but tends to be followed by wild reactions. Collective action generates a certain amount of friction because we can find it violence at varying degrees. So non-cooperation is a action practised by large masses has necessarily to be violent more or less. Gandhi himself witnesses this very fact at several occassions during his own life time, but unfortunately does not recognise the truth.

The peacefulness and passivity of non-cooperation pleaded by Gandhi proceeds from his philosophy of human nature. Man, says Gandhi, is by nature good and peaceful. Here also we find some object of examination. Firstly question arises does human nature possess such an optimistic view. Gandhi himself believes that belonging to animal ancestry, human beings are originally brutes and due to this brute nature one and all always easily choose downword course than the upward.[1] In fact the sanest view of man is that he is neither an angle nor a beast. The great drama of human life consists in the fighting against one's own self with one's own element. Human character is not, the fine flower of a beautiful sentiment, but the hard won fruit of a painful and prolonged conquest. In fact the character of man is not a uniform composition. The world of action is not like the world of ideas free from the laws of motion and friction. Gandhi has made the audacious mistake of trying to annihilate time. He himself accepts that a group of followers of non cooperation may not be non-violent and truthful as an individual because the emphasis in group action tends to shift from inner purity to external confirmity. This is the experience of Gandhi in his life time and as a result he says that mobes have no mind. Thus he contradicts himself his own views of non-cooperation as purely non-violent.

Contradiction comes foreward that on one hand he advocates non-cooperation as non-violent practice based upon human nature, and on the other hand he utters the truth that collective form of men is always pre-dominated by their brute quality and so it is to a greater extent violent. As result mass non cooperation or mass civil disobedience can never be non-violent in nature. Wherever there is slightest presence of violence, it cannot be non-violent. Gandhi, even knowing this truth, never recognise it practically but tries to prove it through the illogical arguments.

To Gandhi non-cooperation is a means of conversion from impure heart to pure one. He once again commits mistake. Here the mistake consists in thinking that this conversion can be done in a short period of limited time. In real sense, there is a gulf between intellectual conviction and moral conversion. The good what we should do, we dos not, but the evil which we should not, that we do. Such misunderstanding of human nature and law of human progress has brought Gandhi to his theory that progress can be achieved by an individual, who are simply instruments. His mistake confirms the man of ideas, who is always a man of good nature. He does not realise the logic of passion, an attribute of a real man.

The revolt of the mass people is in fact the sword that cuts the gordian knot of a quarrel between ruler and ruled. It is the final resort and once the sword of revolt has been unsheathed there must be no looking back. One it is crossed, one and all go and to the bitter and till it is won or lost. Once our feet are set on the path of revolution there must be no turning back. No counting of the cost. No attempt to justify it except by success. But all these truth ought to come before and during the advancement or process of revolution. Ganghi fail's to realise in his progress the very fact in practice of non-cooperation in relation to unrest or revolt. He moves backward and forward in his policy of resistance and make experiments in revolution, whereas the thruth is that in revolution there remains no time for experiments. Revolution is a continuous process of changing society. So it is a natural, social and eternal movement which needs not any experiments, which Gandhi forgets in his thought and practice.

As far as the distinction of non-cooperation and passive resistance is concerned, we clearly find that in view of Gandhi non-cooperation predominantly implies withdrawing of co-ooperation, and civil-disobedience presupposes the habit of willing obedience to laws without fear of their sanctions. Both these are in fact Ganghi's non-violent resistance. But passive resistance has been regarded by Gandhi as the resistance of non-conformists and it covers the suffragette movement. It is regarded as the weapon of the weak and avoids violence.[2] Non-cooperation and civil disobedience differs from passive resistance in three essentials. former is a weapon of the strong, it admits no violence and it ever insists upon truth.[3]

But if we go through these differences we trace out that these differences are not true to the mark. Similar to non-cooperation, passive resistance is also a non-violent method, as says Gandhi. He says that passive resistance occasionaly admits violence. But earlier we have found that Gandhi says, complete non-violence is not possibles then how one can say that non-cooperation or civil disobedience is completely non-violent. Secondly, we have found that non-violence must be in thought, words and deeds, and to harm someone mentally or think to harm someone is also a kind of violence and non-violence because collective and individual acts of violence and non-violence differ in degrees. In his life time Gandhi himself witnesses violence applied by Satyagrahi's during the non-cooperation movement. On the other hand, he says that passive resistance is resistance of non-conformists. It means that non-cooperation is resistance of confirmist. But here also question arises how one can say that non-violent resistance, like non-cooperation is resistance of confirmist. In non-cooperation a resister resists but he never confirms himself that he will succeed. One cannot confirm that the resistance is completely non-violent because there remains difference in mental and physical state of individual and collective actions.

Apart from non-cooperation, Gandhi and after, it has been the fashion to appeal to the authority of Thoreau and others docterinaires

and socially collective action but among all individuals in case of collective action. The truth behind this is that man in society as an individual is never same as we find him in a group or incollective form. One's social behaviour is always diffrent from his behaviour as an individual. The principle underline upon human mind is that social environment and condition make the crowd as such that it losses the ethical fibre of even its basic norms. Crowd can never be sensible and enlightend. Collective action remains under an iron dicipline for a certain period of time under a great stress but later it is followed by wild reaction. It produces a certain amount of friction because it can be found violent in varying degrees. The emphasis in collective action tends to shift from inner purity to external confirmity. Therefore, with his own experience Gandhi says that mobes have no mind. On the one hand he says that civil disobedience either individual or collective, is non-violent based upon human nature, and on the other hand he says that collective form of civil disobedience is predominated by brute quality because there remains violence in its least form, if not in its greater form. But truth is that where ever there is slightest presence of violence it cannot be crowned as non-violence. This fact has been unnoticed by Gandhi himself whether from the legal or the moral point of view. Any collective action whether it may be civil disobedience or some other action is always greater in consequences. It is often said that individual or collective form of individuals has the right to disobey what ever he or they (collective men) find unjustified or against his or their will. But one and all have to do it at his or their own peril, and the state is entitled and bound to punish any infraction of the law. A civil disobeyer can disobey after justified by his own conscience and not of others. This very fact has been forgotten by the advocate of civil disobedience, and as a result the movement of civil disobedience failed during the life time of its advocate.

Civil disobedience has its root in the historical events of human society. There happens some occasions when a man has to result civil disobedience as moral duty to express his disapproval of some laws in the past time of mankind. But the question is under what prevailling conditions of the past a man has to do so. In fact the general exercise of the right to set up one's own conscience above the law whenever any one disapproves of any law engenders a habit of lawlessness and it ends in disruption of the whole society. No state or system can allow each and every one the moral right to be a law into one's own self. In fact it is an gregious mistake to take civil disobedience purely non-violent because the implication of violence or non-implication of violence in no way detracts it from its basic character of a revolutionary movement. It is a crusade against the law, with the object of completely paralysing it, is just as revolutionary as an armed rebellion or a coupd'etat. So civil disobedience must be judged and dealt with by the same standards and methods that are applied to a revolution. So as long as it is possible to secure the fulfilment of every one's aspiration by moral and justified methods, it would be injurious to the best of our interests and to a great extent for humanity, disobedience which is bound to plunge in anarchy and disaster. In real sense the principle of civil disobedience implies the spirit of lawlessness, a mode of law-breaking. And a mass lawlessness can never be checked, whenever an authority wants to do so. It is so because a supporter of lawlessness (in the sense of civil disobedience) always do only what is justified and moral in their own view. Everyone who cares for peace and non-violence supports the forces of law against disobedience and disorder. Thus civil disobedience lacks the complete justification on moral and constitutional ground.

Fasting

Almost all living religions of world sanction fasting as a pious means. But Gandhi uses it as an instrument of political movement. Fasting is, in the view of Gandhi, nothing but a method of *Satyagraha* itself. But it has its own abuses which have been ignored by our great national leader. In the words of Appadorai, "whenever I came across the claim related to fasting in writings of Gandhi, I cannot help in quoting to myself the famous line of Kalidasa, *Vichar Mūṛha Pratiyasi Me Towan.* In light of these words, Gandhi appeared to me to be confounded by anxious thought."[4]

Gandhi himself says that his fast springs from love. If all kind of love can be regarded as coercion, then his fast is also coercion. It is only the way in which a man can fulfil his vow and also relieve himself from strains.[5] But question arises whether it never could flash in Gandhi's mind that the fast is actually pressure, if not direct, some how indirect pressure upon the opponent. It seems simply to give pressure which is infact a kind of black mailing on the cost of one's life. Such pressure is always direct for general mass people.

Fast undertaken directly or indirectly to bring about some change, always have a coercive effect, even though coercion may not be intended. Like all other coercion this sort of un-intented coercion is always undesirable. Satyagraha, says Gandhi, can be practised by individuals and also by the masses. But latter he says that fasting cannot be practised correctly and effectively by the masses. It can be restored only by few selected and qualified individuals. It cannot be undertaken against one's own opponent because it will be a kind of violence. It can be practised against one's heartiest and dearest one's.[6] Here we find clear contradiction in Gandhi's idea (theory) and practice of fasting. Being a form of Satyagraha, it can be practised by one and all, but later he contradicts. It clears the picture that fasting requires pre-qualification. It can always be on individual's practice who are pre-qualified, because if it is practised by unqualified masses, it will prove coercion.

Fasting is a great institution perhaps in all worlds living religions and it is limited to each and every individual's only from religious point of view. Fast is a way infact to devote one's own self towards superior force, 'God'.

But Gandhi takes it as a force or way to convert. It is practised by individual to prove one's own self a true devotee and religious. It is in fact the weakest and simplest way to come near to God. Such kind of fast is not restricted to any individual and also it does not need any previous training except art of devotion. Such kind of fast cannot be practised by a group of people at same place and same time. It is infact subject to each and every individuals.

Fast in Gandhi's opinion is just opposite to its original meaning. He adopts fast, as a religious practice in his own life but later interprets it as way or instrument to practise Satyagraha. He is a staunch follower of Hinduism, specially vaisnavism and uses to practise fast for several religious occasions. But he fails to recognise the sanity and sacredness of the fast and transfers it into a socio political device. Fasting as religious device is to attain God. It is the best way to express love and find self-purification in relation to God and not in Socio-political sphere. But when it is practised against some authority, institution or state, there cannot be any love and self-purification between the two. Fasting as socio-political resort to attain, socio-political gain is infact a selfish end. Fasting as a last resort in the corollary of Satyagraha, never consists love and affection because fast is practised in socio-political arena after a great upheavel. Here real picture comes out that Gandhi commits a mistake in transferring religious norms into political and social practice.

Fasting, as Gandhi assumes, is a pious means of fulfilling one's demand from his superior authority or rulers alien to him. So it implies a pressure on the superior authority or alien rulers. Pressure is a kind of violence, and so fasting is not a pious means. Violence is not pious. Secondly, Fasting is harmful to physical health. Everybody needs to fulfil his own hunger and thrist. It is the basic need of each and every human being. Therefore, fasting is abandoned of fulfilling hunger and thirst, is no less than a poisonous injuction that carries a man to death slowly and swiftly. So it is an indirect means of crime. But Gandhi and the staunch supporters of fasting claim that it is useful for health, both physical and mental. It is a way to attain God which gives a man courage and self-consciousness. But courage and strength never comes without food and drink. It is said, "Health is lost something is lost, and Character is lost every thing is lost". Something includes both body and mind. Every one needs a balance body and mind. Character of anyone always depends on his balance of mind and body. But fasting decreases the strength of mind and body. As a result, with unbalanced bodily and mentally status a man becomes very weak and feels that his mind is slowly becoming void. Thus on the ground of health, fasting is not useful. According to Gandhi, fasting is more successful weapon than human reason to pressurise on the superior authority or alien rulers. Reason has its own limitations which can argue but not necessary to convince any one. But fasting is a threat upon the life of one who adopts it. So it affects the opponent easily. It means fasting is a type of threatening, as good as violence. Thus Gandhi contradicts his own non-violence means or form (i.e. fasting) of a Satyagraha.

Picketing

Peaceful picketing is another way to practise Satyagraha, a non-violent technique to create political and social consciouness. Gandhi takes into account peaceful picketing as the best means to uprise the spirit of swadeshi. Gandhi says that speech is the only weapon and the only way of picketing because it has a great effect and educative value. But on the other hand pleading for fasting. He advocates, that fasting has a great influence because mind of the pepole is not influence through speech and words, for pepole understand only the language of suffering. Here we find clear contradiction in Gandhi's own words. He sometime says that fasting is superior to speech and words and on the other hand he sometime says that speech, words and writing is the only effective weapon of grate educative value. Speech and writing which has great educative inportance in picketing turns to be ineffictive in fasting. It seems that Gandhi himself is unable to deside the right one. No doubt speech and words have a greater value than fasting and also more effective weapen than fasting. Fasting has been already proved a wrong account done by Gandhi. These two weapon of satyagraha differ in its application just like two opposite poles.

By analysing all the forms of satyagraha, we reach to the conclusion that Gandhi being an idealist thinker, doesnot see the inherent contradiction of his own thoughts. All the forms of Satyagraha themselves refute their positive charactor and therefor, the society in which we live becomes a choatic and corrupt one. Contradictions create confusions and confusions beget corruption.

REFERENCES

1. Gandhi, M.K., *Harijan* ,February 1, 1935, p. 410
2. Appadorai, *Political Thought in Modern India,* Vol. I, p. 313-14
3. Appadorai, *Political Thought in Modern India,* Vol. I, p. 296
4. Appadorai, *Political thought of Modern India,* p. 457
5. Gandhi, M.K., *Modern Review,* September 9, 1932 September 11, 1932.
6. Gandhi, M.K., *Harijan,* April 21, 1946, p. 93

6

CONTRADICTIONS IN DIFFERENT ELEMENTS OF SATYAGRAHA

The present chapter attempts to analyse the different elements of Satyagraha adopted by Gandhi, and to show their contradictions inherent. Gandhi starts God and Truth as the fundamental elements of satyagraha. So we should have to examine these two elements at first.

God

For Gandhi, the definitions of God is of no importance because there are innumerable definitions of God, for his manifestations are innumerable.[1] As we have seen in the chapter four, Gandhi identifies God which the dumb poor millions, love and above all truth . Thurth is derived from Sat which means being, and nothing is or existes in reality expect truth. That is why satya or truth is the most important name of God. In fact it is correct to say that truth is God rather than to say that God is Truth.[2] But apart from God as truth God is many other things too. Hence Gandhi terms truth as God and calls it the perfect definition of God.[3] Gandhi conceives God as a person also, because he belives that God is not merely to satisfy the intellect, but also the heart of human beings. Therefore, a man must be able to transform his bad heart into good one, if he could establish his relationship with God. In other words, Gandhi assumes that there exists an interpersonal relation between God and human being, such a relation is possible only when God is conceived as a person.

Being a personal God, He must be attributed with omniscience, omnipotent, omnipresense, all wordly, kind, just, greaseful etc. Attribution to God means the limitation of His infinity. That is way God is finite and so finite God can not be infinity truth. Truth as ultimate reality is absolutely impersonal. Thus Gandhi himself contradicts his own view of God both as person and truth. Person, as wallace depicts,[4] is a human being invested with a certain functions and social character. As well as, a person has a spacific place in the body politic. In other words, personality involves in certain rights, duties and privilages of human kind belongs to a particular society or state.

If personality is the subject of human socio-political rights, duties and privilages, it is very absurd to say that God is a person. We need not to say that God transcends all the conditions of human life. In this respect, personality cannot be applied to God legitimately.

Gandhi is a theist but his theism is of two kinds, Vaishnavism and Advaitism. He believes in personal God as well as absolute Truth. Vaishnavism regards God as ultimate reality where as Advaitism regards truth as ultimate Reality. To Vaishnavism all thing and human beings in the universe are created by God. So all of them are as true as God. To Advaitism, all things and human beings in the world are projection of Brahman 'The Absolute' through Maya. So, the world is unreal. Sankara tries to prove world as real on the empirical ground and terms it ultimately as Adhyas or Vivarta. But Gandhi, being an advatist, calls world as unreal in different sense. He says, "World is changing each and every moment and is, therefore, unreal."[5]

As a Vaishnavite, he also calls world as real, because world is constantly changing process and this process is eternal. What is eternal is real and so Gandhi tries to assimilate both advaitism and vaishnavism. This again contradicts Gandhi's views on God. If world is permanently changing process and thus eternal, it should not be termed unreal. In any respect eternal being is not ureal. Secondly, Gandhi assumes world as real as God, not the vivarta of the Brahman. If God is real, its manifestation or creation can never be unreal. Thirdly, if the universe is unreal, it means all evils including poverty and beggary and injustices done to the human beings are also unreal. In other words, all kinds of evils are non-existent. But Gandhi is not capable of annihilating evils like this way. If he can, he do never way that human beings should change their evil spirits (hearts) into good one. Thus Gandhi proves himself inconsistant and this inconsistancy prevails, because of his assumption of God both as personal as well as impersonal. In fact, he emphasises impersonal God as Reality (Truth). But his lust to personal God to never doomed. In his views personal God is essential for those persons who need his touch, and a devotee can establish personal communication with him. For Gandhi, there is no distinction between Truth and God as such. His statement "Truth is God and God is

Truth", claims this fact. This statement consists of two propositions.

(i) Truth is God.
(ii) God is Truth

Both proportions are universal affirmative and in Barbara mood in first figure. Therefore, these propositions are truth in form. However, there lies contradiction in them. Truth is the subject and God is the predicate in first proposition; Whereas God is the subject and Truth is the predicate in second proposition. A predicate expresses adjective or attributes of a subject. So both God and Truth have been termed as attribute of truth and God respectively. In other words as subject both truth and God are nouns. According to grammer both noun and adjective cannot be synonums. If God or truth is attribute,It is not possible for him or It to be a subject or noun. Thus, ambiguity prevails in the conception of God as truth or truth as God. This ambiguity or contradiction can also be elaborated in other way. If truth is the sole reality, neither subject nor object can be outside of it. Self consciousness is another state of pure consciousness. The determinate God is the determination of the indeterminate one. To explain the experience of change, time and creation, Gandhi brings in the personal God. But since truth is abstract, transcendental, changeless, formless, impersonal and indeterminate, both truth and God can be declard mere phenomena. Here we find Gandhi's non-dualistic thought and, God fails to bridge the gulf between the dualism of formless and formed.

Gandhi strongly proves himself as a trust in one of his articles.[6] He says "My Rama is not the historical Rama, the son of Dashratha but the eternal, unborn, the one without a second. Him alone I worship". He establishes that Rama, Ishvara and Allah are all the names of God. But Rama is an incarnation of God in Hindu mythology. Incarnation is not God in toto, but projection of God. To be a projected God and God as truth are different. A projected God or Rama is not a transcendental being but a finite being. He is considered as God for his good qualites. So incarnation is an indication of being a man good. It means Rama as increation of God is not perfect and imperfect (incarnated) God is not absolutely truth. Going through Gandhi's conception of God we reveal that Gandhi never gives due regard to reason in formulating his ideas. He often talks about, "The inner voice," or "the voice of the conscinsce." this is the fact that he appers to be convinced about the veracity of his beliefs on the testimony of his own inner voice. Rationalist are admirable but rationalism is a hideous monster. When it claimes omnipotence for itself, attribution of omnipotence to reason is as bad as a piece of idolatory as the worship of stick and stone believing it to be God[7]. These all proves that Gandhi does not emphasise on rational demonstration of God's existence. His God can be known only by inner realisation, by sincere and sacred inner experience.

But in the course of examination we have to go through some evidences regarding the existence of God. All such arguments are not directly given by Gandhi, but are inherent in his ideology. The collection of his writings on Hinduism, we can trace some arguments like Cosmological or causal accepted by Gandhi. He says 'God is the uncaused cause'of the universe. If universe is effect and God is its cause a question must arise that whether God creates himself. There is no answer of this question. According to the law of causation every events must have a cause. God has no cause because if one can try to find out the cause of God, he has to walk continuously without a moment rest. Thus the argument preys in the fallacy of infinite regress. To save the argument from the fallacy of infinite regren, a theist like Gandhi steps his argument with God as ultimate cause of the universe. According to moral argument, all actions good or bad have their own fruits. Man is the doer who cannot give judgement upon his actions. So an infinite eternal being must crist for performing the task of giving reward or punishment to human beings in accordance with their actions. That infinite eternal being is God. This argument characterises God as a justice. A Justice is a powerful man having the right of decision on any legal matter. So moral argument is a form of legal one and here we can find a contradiction.

Morality is an ideal. It belongs to the verb 'ought'. But law is a fact. It belongs to the verb 'is'. There is a great difference between ought' and 'is'. 'Ought' is never fulfilled but near to fulfilment. 'Is' itself is a fulfilment. Secondly, if God is kind, He should not punish anyone; because punishment given by Him refutes His kindness who always regards forgives. Forgiveness is a good deed whereas punishment is a bad one. If God punishes any human being, it means God himself is not kind and his cruelty contradicts His good nature. But no theist including Gandhi refute the good nature of God.

Gandhi, like James, finds practical nature in assumption of God's Sex intense. When a man falls in misery or in trouble, he resolts the path of praying God and gains the strength to fight his misery. But the pragmatic argument is not satisfactry. It is not essential that by praying God, a man must have strength to fight the strife and misery of life. This is mere belief without reason and so Gandhi is unable to prove the existance of God with all arguments including pragmatic. Like all other schools and sects Gandhi also believes without question that it is God's spiritual power which has created the universe. There is a difference of opinions about God's form, nature, and His relation with universe. Every religion claims itself fine and it alone knows the reality. But Gandhi tries to solve the problem. For this he asserts that every religion is true in the sense that all of them conceive one almighty God. He gives stand to his philosophy upon religious connection and never attempt to asses any one of them in the light of reason and logic. In whole philosophy of Gandhi, specially his God, we can easily draw that he is inspired by different schools of Indian philosophical tradition, and interprets them in his own way. As the idealism of Gandhi is based upon theology, it is altogether different from the idealism of Plato and Berkeley. Plato says that concept are objective realities, which he coins ideas. Theses ideas of things, the absolute ultimate reality from which all things is explained.[8]

According to Barkeley reality consists of spirits and their ideas only. His famous axions, 'Esse ist Percipi' and of percipi means essence of any thing in principle consists of ideas.[9] Gandhi can be classed as an objective idealist of an old fashioned and classical type, as he also believes that God pervades in all thing of this world whether living or non-living. This very belief arises a serious question, if God is immanent in all the things of this world shall be just and there shall be no imperfection in them. Gandhi has also accepted the doctrine of Hegel that whatever is rational is real. Here again in relation Gandhi question arises, if real is rational and rational is real, than what will happen to Gandhi's ideas of social, religious and political reconstruction with help of non-violent resistance for our socio-political institutions are also the reflection of that universal soul. Therefore, there is no scope left to change them, as they are perfect in themselves. To solve this puzzle Gandhi also advocates whatever we perceive is simply perception of our mental state which is simply to fly in the face of all evidence and disolves the material universe into an unsubstantial dream. In such a case we are compelled to admit the objects as a part from our knowledge. The fact we perceive in an object does not mean that it is true. Gandhi takes the basic principles of experiences and declares that whatever is bound by space and time, and casuality can not real. He accepts the world as Maya and terms it as appearence. No doubt Gandhi tries to a great extent to solve the riddle of real and rational but also creates another problem. That is, if we regard universe as appearence, we have to accept all the evils injustices and poverty of the world simply as appearence. Getting himself confused of real and rational, leaving the slippery ground of idealism he accepts dualism. Thus he favours at a time both Absolutism (Monism) and Dualism. As well as he accepts pluralism in the concept of world as Maya.

Following monism, dualism and pluralism, Gandhi's hotch-potch of thought leaves no room for any systematic and logical principle. It is true that he is not an academician , but his great lacuna is that he does not follow even simple logic. He mystifies philosophy which is very difficult to be accepted and aserted by this present unbelieving age. Infact the whole philosophy of Gandhi in relation to God is neither fully idealistic nor dualistic because he tries to reconcille the two. His whole effort of reconciliation is based fully upon relligious speculations, which is neither logical nor scientific and experimental.

Truth

In philosophical analysic of Mahatma Gandhi God is the most important aspect. But truth has its own importance in his whole philosophical tradition because both, truth and God are two sides of the same coin. Truth is in fact the key stone of his entire ethical philosphy. He tries to establish that there is no religion higher then truth and he accepts truth as the ultimate moral standard and coined God as truth. He understands truth in spiritual sense and indentifies it with God.

Metaphysically truth is an ultimate reality and theologically it is God. Thus Gandhi's statement 'Truth is God and God is truth' assimilates metaphysics with theology. Gandhi attempts to identify epistemology with both metaphysics and theology when he says that true knowledge means knowledge of God as well as that of from moral view point he accepts truth as truthfulness. Truthfulness is a part and parcel of goodness, and Goodness or truthfulness is totaly vested in the perfect one, none but God is perfect. Thus Gandhi reaches to the conclusion that in all the three senses (metaphysically, epistamologically or moraly) truth is nothing but God. But ultimately he prefers the word truth to God, as we have alrady seen in the previous pages. An atheist cannot deny the power and necessity of truth. Gandhi defines truth as the voice within one's heart, but this definition of truth cannot be free from confusions. In fact, Gandhi has not defined truth in technical way. Truth infact refers to existing fact or ideals which do not exist. Truthfulness is agreement of ideas with words, and of words with fact. But Gandhi used truthfulness in the sense of fearless pursuit of truth as an ideal, and been actualise as an ideal truth, as fact. He thinks, by free actions of human beings, ideal is such which can never be actualised but it can reach nearer to fact. This is great differance between facts and ideals. Facts are objective experiences or observations of human beings, they are not utopian. Ideals are merely utopia. They are subjective mental goal, and this subjectivity differs from man to man. Objectivity is unified and both unification and differentiation have their own different nature. So it is quite impossible to assimilate the two with each other or bridge the gap between them.

Gandhi tries to establish God as one and only truth who is also the only true knowledge and all goodness exists in him. He also says that we have many bodies but have one soul that is the truth only. But both truth and untruth are moral standards which exists in every human heart. Gandhi only accounts good aspects of human hearts. He believes that being an offsprings of God or truth, all human beings are naturally good. But he forgets the basic nature of human being. Basically or by nature a man is always consists of both goodness and badness (evil). If a man is basically good, there should not be any kind of evils in society. Now here we find several kind of evil doers, i.e. criminals thieves etc. But we have all these types of persons in our society, which clears that Gandhi's view is partial.

Truth has a relative value because it is a relative phenomena. it has a relative validity within space and time without any form. Truth exists in the human mind, where truth and untruth are infact man made moral standards. Truth is related to untruth in the same way as good in related to evil. If we term truth as God then God also bacomes relative because where there is truth, there always remains possibility of untruth, for attainment of truth in this world it is necessary to recognise untruth. Without distinction betweeen the two we can not recognise what and where truth is. If truth is infinite and transendental, the only evidnce of truth is inner conscience or inner voice of human being. Here a problem lies that it inner conscience is the only evidence of truth, it has a great difficulty to solve the problem of different conceptions of truth coined by different thinkers. Gandhi himself realises this difficulty when he admits that what may be truth for one may be untruth for another.[10] Regarding this differance Gandhi maintains that human mind works through innumerable media and that the evolutoin of human mind is not the same for all.[11] The answer given by him is not quite satisfactory.

If truth is an ultimate reality, it means there is one and only one truth named God. If there is only one truth and all creations belongs to it, it is must that the universe also be true in every aspect. In other words no lie should prevail in the universe, and therefore, nobody should be a lier. But what our experience is in fact beyond this hypothesis. The universe has both truthful and untruthful human beings. Secondly, truth in human personality is absolutely subjective. What is true for a person is untrue for others, as Gandhi himself admits. Therefore, there is no objective truth. Without objectively no truth can be termed as ultimate reality. Thus Gandhi's conception of truth or God itself bellies (vanishes).

But being a practical thinker, as some scholors call him, he does not want to prove himself as an unsuccessful thinker regarding conception of truth. He despite of assuming an absolute truth as ultimate reality, coins truth as relative too. Through relative truth he tries to slove the problem mentioned in the previous paragraph.

According to him, truth as a relative phenomena, a this wordly concept (not a universal concept) is different for different individuals. If truth varies from person to person, it can not be accepted as God. Further more if we accept the truth not one but more than one varying as perils degree from one to another it seems plurality of truth. Plurality of truth defies the concept of one almighty God. In other words we can say that truth cannot be termed as God.

Gandhi attempts to conquor all these difficulties with saying that then ordinary man cannot reach truth in an ordinary way. In his own words, "we have the belief based upon experience, that those who would make individual search after truth as God must go through several vows, as for instance the vow of truth, the vow of *ahimsa* etc. Truth is not the inner vioce of all but of few persons who practices these vows.[12] These words of Gandhi are also leading to contradiction. We have all ready seen in the previous chapter that Gandhi tries to establish truth is each and every human heart. We also know that other thinkers say that God resides in each and every human heart in form of soul. In the same way Gandhi says that truth is God and He resides in each and every soul. But in his above statement he contradicts himself by accepting truth as inner voice of the few. In addition to it he terms truth as a vow to attain God. It means that God is an end and truth is its means. Thus truth cannot be indentified with God .In this way Gandhi contradicts his own conception of God as truth or truth as God. Truth is secondary to God ,but Gandhi does not believe it and here lies contradiction in his concept of truth. Gandhi opines that God is an ultimate unity because all worldly phenomena are His manifestations, so all contrary aspects and confusions have merged into God, or to say, God is the unification of all. Contradictions prevails in the universe. If this is the position of God, it must lead to limit His absoluteness. Absolute God should be pure and non-qualified. Unification of all contradictory is idle a quality with quality and in such a case God has to leave His original nature of absolute truth as mentioned by Gandhi. Therefore, God as an ultimate unity is a mere idea. It is not essential that an idea must transform into fact. So Gandhi is not capable of proving the existence of truth or God, but he accepts truth or God as an idea only. Idea can be transformed into belief or faith, but not into reality. Hance Gandhi's views on truth and God seems to be a neoplatonic idea. Gandhi accepts God as only real knowledge, and also says that God is unknowable. An imperfect man like Gandhi determines God's unknowability, and on the other hand he himself establishes God as the ultimate knowledge. About unknowable, no body is able to determine. If any body says that there is an unknowable entity like God, it implies that there is a knowledge that someting exists. So there is no question of unknowability. Thus an idea of unknowable God has been perished. Mahatma Gandhi tries to reconcile the contradictory ideas of absolute power of truth and freedom of will. But this reconciliation is not acceptable. Gandhi asserts that God is responsible for both good and evil action. He directs assassin's dagger no less than a surgeon's knife. So human being are mere instrument to perform good or bad deeds instructed by God and therefore, there is no importance of vows. In the true sense good and evil action are inclind out and out to human purpose. Therefore, it is not untrue to say that man is the creator of good and evil. Several thinkers also have studied and concluded that evil is not a part of the one, the God or truth, but it is man made. If evil is to be attaracted as a attribute to God, the existence of God may be ceased because evil and good are qualities which limits God and reduces him to a person. Thus truth and untruth as good and bad respectively in their moral sense can not be attributed to God. In other words, truth as the highest good or as a moral principle is not applicable to God, as the highest principle.

Truth by its nature is also closely connected with knowledge. When knowledge of a thing is attained, human intellect feels compelled to inquire whether knowladge so attaind is equivalent to truth or truth is a quality which when added to knowledge transforms into being true. This nature of relationship between truth and reality has been variously understood by thinkers of realist, idealist and pragmatist schools, with or wothout any metaphysical prediction. As a consequence truth has sometimes been equated with reality in some sense and sometimes reality has been thought of as wider then truth. In general,

the cult of non-violence.[16] The spirit of people had got to be respected one should not attempt to thwart the aspiration of the masses. So one and all must formulate all the principles and programme in clear language and realise it by the wide spread and militant use of direct action by working masses. Although it will be stupid to talk of premature violence, we are nevertheless of the opinion that non-viloent movement or revolution is and impossibility.[17] On the other hand, ethically non-violence as a cult is immoral, because it suppresses the basic nature of human beings. Suppression is nothing but exploitation, is the worst type of violence. The cult of non-violence is the opposite of what it appears to be. It offers a direct aid to violence in practice because in practice of non-violence there one can find out very clearly that, "there one's choice stands not between violence and non-violence, but between violence practised for ages, for enslaving, exploiting, tyrannising multitude of human beings, and possible obligatory use of violence for the liberation of slaves, for the assertion of human rights and for putting end to violence.[18] In relation to Gandhi non-violence has also very close relation to Hinduism. Roy remarks that it is not to be belived that non-violence is inherent in the Hindu antiquity. No sensible man can possibly believe that non-violence is inherent in Hindu humanitarianism, so long as Rama, Krishana, Arjuna, Bhima etc. are the ideals of Hindu manhood.[19] Criticising Gandhi's idea on non-violence, Lajpat. Rai also says that non-violence of Gandhi is not a truth but it is a fad.[20] Rai belongs to the Jaina family, asserts that his grandfather was staunch follower of Jaina's cult of non-violence, though he was businessman. Being businessman his grandfather considred all kinds of trickeries in trade and business as only valid as will as good too. It means that according to Rai it is not necessary for a man to follow non-violence in practice, in accordance with his theoretical belief in it (non-violence). But the principle of non-violence must be practised in thought and action as well Gandhi himself violates this rule when he advises to kill the calf. If the killing of a calf is not violent or immoral act, it implies that Gandhi's non-violence requires some kind of immoral or violent act too, we can understand it with an example. There are several incurable diseases from which human beings suffer. According to Gandhian thought of non-violence, all these people should be poisoned. If someone takes life of a man who is too old or suffering form incurable disease, it should not be treated as a murder. None of religious or ethical philosophy advocates such act as moral and non-violent. Being a staunch supporter of vaisnavism, Gandhi abuses us by advising of killing the ill calf. On the one hand he says that to think of killing or giving injury to someone is violent and on the other hand he advocates to take life of a living being. From humanitarian point of view it is also one's duty to serve such being who are suffering and near to death. To think of killing or taking life of a living being before he dies his own death is immoral,violent and cruel act. Such act is against the law of nature and man cannot go against the nature. We are also a part of this vast mystic nature. If we cannot give life to someone, we have no right to take life of someone,even he is counting his days due to some unvoidable cause. But Gandhi's advise to kill the ill calf has a good intentaion of liberating it from unbearable suffrings. It means that ends justifies the means. But this is not acceptable because justification depends on means and if means are violent, ends naturally be a violent act, or vice-versa.

Clarence Marsh beautifully cleared the contradictory elements inherent in Gandhian non-violent. He contrasts non-violence with violence by saying that non-violence coercion is and ought to be a two edged sword. If causes and it is will that it should cause inconvenience and suffering to those who wield it as well as to those against whom it is invoked. It is exactly contrary to violent methods, for a principal reason accounting for the appeling growth of terrorism in modern times, is the unfortunate fact that the development of fire arms and high explosive carries no automatic check and penalty for all who use them. As for the non-violence the people stands more or less in a position to determine which way the blow shall fall, who or which party shall suffer the greater loss.[21]

Anthony De Crespigny in his article entitled, 'The nature and methods of non-violence' gives a scientific analysis of non-violence. He defines non-violence as an attempt to limit or destroy freedom of choice which does not involve the threat or use of physical force.[22]

Arthur Moore criticizes the high spiritual claim made for the non-violence of Gandhi, saying that it draws a spiritual distinction between physical and mental violence. It is a method which is open to unarmed people and is on a par with boycott and strike which are indeed part of its technique. But it is not a distinctively spiritual one. The Economic object of boycotting, a form of non-violent practice is to provide work wages and food for one set of pepole and to deprive another set of work wages and food. Between starving and killing there is no moral difference.[23] An eminent British Marxist Dr. Johan Lewis very frankly comments speaking of Gandhi's non-violent that it is a form of (compulsion) and as such (arouse resentment). Morality in fact becomes a form of violence, even it is not physical violence.[24]

Raising a question, conversion or compulsion, Nehru, the most rewarded disciple of the Mahatma says that whatever the motives of conversion behind non-violence is in practice, it has been a powerful weapon for compulsions as well, thuogh that compulsion is practised or exercised in the most civilised and least objectionable manner. There is line between non-violance and violance. Compulsion and conversion often enough moral force is a more terrible coercive factor than physical violance.[25]

Appart from all, Dr. K. Satchidananda Murthy alleges that the Gandhian conception of non-violance is in fact not a case of genuine non-violance, for it cannot be founded on national interests but only on universalism.[26]

Mahatma Gandhi sees marality of non-violance rooted in the nature of man becouse moral valuse are not related to the socio-cultural condition of a particular time. What is right and what is wrong are conceptions which man has evolved for his own benefit in million of years spent in the struggle for existance. The conception of right and wrong consequently differs not only with countries and race but also with the change of times in the history of some nation or race. This very fact is completely over looked in Gandhi's non-violance. He forgets the psychology of conscience. Conscience infact is abscure in psychological origin and misleading in its dictates. Inalienable judgements moral and immoral, violent and non-violent are passed with most assurance by the unreflective and ill informed who have neither the wit nor the interest to care about the consequences of action.[27]

Gandhi account's non-violence as end as well as means, to attain an end. An end is an ideal. Both the ideal and instrument cannot be the same. An instrument is in fact an ideal to be actualised in fact. Actual and to actualised are not same things or processes. Gandhi also feels this difficulty , so he takes resolt with amystic languge to solve this difficulty. According to him both non-violence and violence depends upon god. God therefore, alone knows the intention of man. In this regard non- violence is both an end and a means at the same time. What is an act of violence should not be avoided for it may be an act of non-violence. Gandhi's answer as mystic may be justifiable, but it does not provide a sound basis for a social philosophy. If it is God who alone knows the intention of man, this cuts the very root of the Gandhian non-violence both as a means and an end. Violence becomes non-violence at the will of god, otherwise there is no distinction between violence and non-violence. In the case it is absolutely unanswerable to distinguish the society is full of chaos. Gandhi has also often taken the consequence into consideration. He revises his doctrine of non-violence so many times that his ideals are generally confusing. He says somethings at one place and opposes the very things at another. For instance he says that complete non-violence is impossible because man in imperfact and so some violence is essential for his existence.

According to Namboodaripad, "For Gandhi truth, morality and *ahimsa* (non-violence) are not absolutely, but relative".[28] Regarding contradictory and confusing ideology of the Mahatma, Pt. Nehru comments that Gandhi's thoughts is a bit obscure. I am not clear in himself. One step is enough for me he (Gandhi) says, and does not try to look into the future or to have a clearly conceived end before him.[29] For non-violance, Gandhi says, look after the means and the end will take care of itself. He never tireds of repeating the same. Be good in personal and individual life, and rest will follow. Nehru says it is not scientific attitude or perhaps ethical attitude. It is narrowly moralist and beg the question, what is goodness, in merely an individual or a social affair.[30]

Gandhi unfortunately makes morality an individual affiar. He does not go deep into the implication of good means for good ends. Here the choice is not between good and imperfect (bad) means. The choice is between less violance than complete violance. Any act moral or immoral, violent circumstances in which it takes place. Though Gandhi says, "Man is the measure of every thing and yet crucify man at the alter of fixed means. He denies the ordinarily accepted theory that laws (means) are made for man and not men for laws (means) . Laws can be changed if they do not guarantee the welfare of human being.

Non-violence of Gandhi is in no way complete and perfact in itself, says Rajneesh. It is weak and incomplete in itself. Non-violence of Gandhi is only for a sole objective called supperession. In the opinion of Rajneesh suppression is also a kind of violence.[31] Where ever there is a kind of preassure either direct of indirect,there exists violence, either by taking dharna or fasting in front of someone's house with a condition that accept the will of the satyagrahi or he will kill himself. The way one puts pressure may be non-violent but pressure in itstlf is violent in nature. This act of violence is too much microscopic because if we threat someone to take his life he will fight and resist upto his strength, but if we threat to kill ourselves the opponent gets no way to escape, except to agree upon the terms.

Non-violence of Gandhi would be completly non-violent if it is not known to even our neighbours about our act and objective. Non-violent act means to be complete passive, and alone calling that almighty through prayer and meditation for one's betterment, even he is one's opponent. Non-violence does not mean that people might know the fact and come forward to save one's life and resister becomes subject of the media. This is a kind of violence because it is a transformed aspect of violence.[32] Non-violence does not do anything but the change comes in it in its due course. Inspite of life long research on non-violence Gandhi never takes into account the practicabilty of non-violence and also never take a firm stand on the specific way of non-violence among its different grades in theory and practice. He takes it in a peculiar way to justify his thought and practice.

Swadeshi

Swadeshi, as Gandhi means is a movement of self country made things or belonging to one's own country. In other sense it is a movement of patriotism. Patriotism is synonyms to nationalism. But Gandhi, as a humanitarian, does not limit his *Swadeshi* movement to only one's country. His conception of Swadeshi is farwide and internationalised. Thus, Swadeshi includes both nationlism and internationlism, and here lies contradiction.

Nationalism, in general sense,is a political principle that concentrates itself on the nation only. A person who serves and sacrifices himself for the cause of his own nation is designated as nationalist. But, to Gandhi it is not nationalism. To him, nationlism is the principle that intends to serve humanity. Nationalism and patriotism are almost the same principle. Therefore patriotism is also on the service of humanity. If any body does not serve for the cause of humanity, he is never a nationalist. In Gandhi's words,"a patriot is so much the patriot if he is a luckwarm humanitarian."[33] Thus Gandhi's nationalism is liberal, not rigid. Due to his liberal attitude towards nationalism, he is ready without any hesitation to take help from the foreign capital and talents to promote home industry in every field, i.e. technology and science, medicine, agriculture, etc. But he has the condition to utilise the foreign aids. He wants that foreign capital and talents must be under the effective control of his own country. This liberalism of Gandhi leads to internationalism. Not only this feature but other features of Gandhian nationalism also lead to internationalism. Therefore, Gandhi says that without nationalism there is no way to reach internationalism.

The other feature of Gandhian nationalism is that it promotes the importation of foreign goods to our country. According to Gandhi, the people should inport only those essential goods which cannot be manufactured in the country. Importation of such goods should not effect the national economy of the indigenous trade and occupation.[34]

The third feature of Gandhian nationalism is to make India self dependent in its economic areana. Nationalism, through home industries, plans to provide employment to millions and starving people of the country. All the people, starting their own home industries, becomes self dependent and are able to fulfil their daily essential necessities. Moreover, the positive implication of Swadeshi is though centred on the local people and their problems, it must follow that all local people of the country or the world have stood to solve their problems on their feet, and thus the whole of the nation and the universe become equally sound in their economic aspect. Therefore it is said that the principle of Swadeshi, in its positive form, is not based on narrow and regional consideration as M.N. Roy blames.[35] If every makes use of the locally produced goods, all the goods produced in the world will be locally consumed. Roy blames nationalism as on antagonist to human freedom or the individual's personality. In his words," Nation is a metaphysical concept, yet the human beings, of flesh and blood, must sacrifice everything to make the nation great and glorious. That is the essence of nationalism. That is to, sacrifice, a reality at the alter of fiction, of and illusion."[36]

But this blame on nationalism is not true regarding Gandhian nationalism. Gandhi always prefers individual freedom to the nation. He says "My love, of nationalism is that my country may become free, that if need be the whole of the country may die, so that the human race may live. There is no room for race hatred there. Let that be our nationalism."[37] This statement of Gandhi shows the humanitarian attitudes inherent in Gandhian nationalism. In other words Humanism is necessarily involved in it. Nationalism emphasises that every village or the nation must be self supporting and self contained unit exchanging only such necessities with other village or nation as are not locally produced. "Just as the cult of patriotism (Nationalism) teaches as today", Gandhi observes, "the individual has to die for the family, the family has to die for the village, the village for the district, the district for the province, and the province for the country, and even so has country has to be free in order that it may die, if ncecessary , for the benefit of the world."[38]

Thus, nationalism of Gandhi is not absolutely limited but to some extent wide. In fact, it is the first step of entering internationalism. Internationalism, as Gandhi himself realises, is possible only when nationalism become a fact, that is, when pepole belonging to the different countries have organised themselves and are able to act as one man. This unitary membership of the universe is internationalism in the sense of Gandhi.

Internationalism in the sense of Gandhi is nothing but the old Indian principle of the universe as one family Vasudhaiva Kutumbakam. The universe, in Gandhi diffrent countries are its members. So there must be cooperation, sympathy, tolerance, mutual help among all the countries. It fallows disarmament and peace among all the countries. Thus Gandhian internationalism suggests peace and disarmament for the whole univers. On the ideal plane it is good, but on the real plane it is impossible, because a man, even Gandhi, cannot be an internationalist if he is not a nationalist. Nationalism rather limits the end of the human beings. The feeling of Nationalism essentially brushes up the feeling of internationalism or vice-versa. If a man is an internationalist or a nationalist in the Gandhian sense, he is free to import some goods that he needs. Importation of goods from other countries is gradually converted into smuggling. If a country agrees to purchase some goods which it needs from the other country, the seller must exploit the purchaser. So smuggling and exploitation are esentially underflowing the Gandhian internationalism. That is why our country or society is full of smugglers, black marketers and exploiters. This leads our society into chaotic conditions which are the implication of negative aspect inhrent in Swadeshi. In fact, the Gandhian concept of Swadeshi is not a fact but a utopia only. A utopian principle does never perform a good task to society. This is perhaps the cause of failure of Gandhian movement of Khadi and Swadeshi after independance in Indian society.

The internationalism of Gandhi brings the fashion of the west in the east. As Gandhi supports the use of foreign goods if they not be harmful to home industries, it flows rapidly to use foreign goods in our Indian society. All of us forget the clause which Gandhi emphasises, "not harmful to home industries." The clause which Gandhi emphasises is absoutely hypothetical because it lacks the courage of universalising nationalism in its true sense. Instead, it popularises internationalism as a negative implication of Swadeshi. As a result, our present society becomes a greater pauper than that in the pre-British era.

Thus, Swadeshi as a moral value, the corollary of Satyagraha, has adversely affected our society today. In reality, the misconception of Swadeshi is the sole reason of this effect. If all of us could use the concepts of nationalism and internationalism preached by Gandhi in their real aspect, the positive one, our society becomes most pious and peaceful, as desired by Gandhi. Untill we being true followers of Gandhi, do not balance both nationalism and internationalism, as Gandhi disires, we are quit unable to serve our country or society and even humanity. Swadeshi, in the real sense of Gandhi is the movement of service to humanity. This is the worthiest implication of Swadeshi depicted by Gandhi, and all of us today should use it for saving our society from destruction.

REFERENCES

1. Gandhi, M.K., *Autoboigraphy,* p. 7.
2. Gandhi, M.K., *Yeravada Mandir,* p. 1.
3. Gandhi, M.K., *Bapu's Letters to Mira,* p. 189.
4. Wallace, *Lectures and Essays in Natural Theology and Ethics,* p. 267.
5. Gandhi, M.K., *Young India,* January 28, 1926.
6. Gandhi, M.K., *Harijan,* April 28, 1946.
7. Lal, B.K., *Contemporary Indian Philosophy,* p. 98.
8. Stace, *The Critical History of Greek Philosophy,* W.T., p. 186.
9. Masih, Y., *Story of Modern Philosophy,* p. 182.
10. Gandhi, M.K., *Young India,* 1931, pp. 427-28.
11. Gandhi, M.K., *Young India,* 1931, pp. 427-28.
12. Gandhi, M.K., *Harijan,* February 20, 1937.
14. Bradely, *Essays on Truth and Reality,* p. 114.
14. Roy, M.N., *One Year of non-cooperation,* Calcutta, 1923.
15. Roy, M.N., *Political Letters,* Zurich, 1924, pp. 29-30.
16. Roy, M.N., *Political Letters,* Zurich, 1924, pp. 29-30.
17. *Ibid.*
18. Roy, M.N., *Heresies of the 20th century,* Vol-I, p. 37.
19. Roy, M.N., *Fragments of a Prisoners Diary,* Vol-I, p.37.
20. Rai Lajpat, *Modern Review,* July 1916.
21. Philosophy of Mahatma Gandhi, p. 331-32 cited in Bhattacharya, B.D., "*Political Philosophy*".
22. *Political Studies,* London, Vol-XII, No. 2, June 1964, pp. 256-165.
23. The evolutaion of Mr. Gandhi is S. Radhakrishnan's *Mahatma Gandhi—Eassays and Raflections*; by Moore, Arthur.
24. Lewis, *The Modarn Quarterly,* Johan.,Vol-I, No.2, p. 59.
25. *Allahabad Law Journal,* Nehru, J.L., Soviet Russia, 1928, cited in B.D. Bhattacharya's, "*Political Philosophy of M. Gandhi*, p. 336.
26. *Political Philosophy of M. Gandhi,* Bhattacharya, B., pp. 334-35 by K. Satchidananda Murthy.
27. Lewis, J., *The Modern Quartile,* vol-1, no-2, p. 59.

28. Namboodripad, E.M.S., *Mahatma and The Ism,* p. 124.
29. Nehru, J.L., *Nehru on Gandhi,* pp. 90-91.
30. Nehru, J.L., *Nehru on Gandhi,* p. 90-91.
31. Rajneesh, *Karmayoga,* Osho., pp. 211-13.
32. Rajneesh, *Karmayoga Dharma Aur Gandhi,* Osho., pp. 211-13.
33. Gandhi, M.K. *Young India,* March 16, 1921, p. 81.
34. Patil, S.H., *Gandhi and Swaraj.*
35. Ojha, V.N., *M.N. Roy: His Philosophical Ideas,* p. 206.
36. Roy, M.N. & Spartt, *Beyond Communism to Humanism,* p. 132.
37. Shreeman, *The Vioce of Truth,* p. 248.
38. Narayan, S., *The Vioce of Truth,* pp. 247-248.

7

NEGATIVE IMPLICATIONS OF SATYAGRAH IN OUR SOCIETY AND ITS EFFECT

As I have analysed elements and forms of Satyagraha in the preceding chapters and found out their inherent contradictions, it implies that Satyagraha as a socio-political theory is contradictory in its character. Contradictions confuse human mind, and confused mind is unable to take right decisions to act. So a society, consists of human beings, is itself confused. Confusion creates chaos and anarchy. We, all members of our present existing society feel this chaotic and anarchic situation. Here I attempt to search out the root cause of this socio-political chaotic and anarchic situation of our contemporary society. Before finding out the root cause, it is necessary to enumerate the present situation of our socio-political and religious condition of our society.

Being a member of Indian society, I feel that the present situation of our country is too much grimed. The basic nature and character of the present social setup is clearly reflected by its on going thoughts and actions, i.e. egoism, bribery, lieness, rape and murder, smuggling, mass movements, terrorism etc. Now a day Egoism and Bribery has become the basic norm of our socio-political life. Each and every member of our society is absolutely self centred. One and all want to fulfil their own desires. For the purpose, to achieve their aim, they can do any shameless job with their fellow beings, there is no good samaritan in our contemporary society. Apart from egoism, bribery has become a common act done by one and all. Our present society has accepted it as a cult, not as a immoral act. This is the outcome of egoist nature of our social beings for fulfilment of one's own end bribery is the way adopted by the working class of our social setup.

Though bribery is an unconstitutional cult of our society, it has been stamped morally in disguise by our ruling class. These people (with a very few exceptions) are the foremost bribers. But they have and art to pose themselves as honest persons berfore their ruled. It means that our social system is corrupt from top to bottom, because there is a proverb that as the ruler, so the people. Our society is of no character or in other words characterless because the character of the people in any society is the projection of that of their rulers.

Above to all the said social evils the most prominent and invogue are the crimes like murder, rape, mass robbery and terrorism. Present society has adopted the impure means to attain its end instead of the pious one. Our egoist character take us to these evil acts not permisible by any religion, or law. Today our society is a mute spectator or rape, murder, dacoity, terrorist act etc. In every corner, every time, and seems a general phenomena of our total social and political setup. No doubt these all acts are nothing but the forms of violent act.

Thus now we live in a society which is full of violence and immorality. Mahatma Gandhi always tries to keep the society away from all these impure and immoral acts. His movements of Satyagaha is also one of his weapons to make our society pure and moral. But he is unable to see the negative implication of his Satyaraha movement. As I have already said in the second chapter that Satyagraha means the firmness in truth. Truth is the basic principle of all Gandhian thoughts. Truth is always one and only one. It is absolute, formless and undivided ultimate reality. Even then he believes in two kinds of truth-absolute and relative. Relative truth is nothing but an expression of the absolute truth. However, both are different in thier character, if truth is one and only one, it is never possible to divide it into absolute and relative one. If truth is of two kinds, it is impossible to coin absolute truth as only ultimate reality. This is the fault of Gandhi. He has also confused truth as metaphysical, epistemological, moral as well as theological. Being a metaphysical entity truth is only truth either absolute or relative.

Epistemologically, truth is itself knowledge. As moral beings truth is truthfulness and theologically, truth is God. Thus in view of Gandhi there is no difference among truth, God, knowledge and truthfulness. All these terms are abstract, but in character they are not the same. Truth is inactive and impersonal. God is active and personal. Creation depends upon God,not on truth. Being and ultimate reality truth can never create the world. It has to take the help of God to perform its duty of creation. So there should be a mediatory source between truth-

and God. According to advaita vedanta, this mediatory source is maya. Gandhi does not believe in maya. So he says, like Vishishtadvaita Vedanta, that truth itself is able to create the world. It should not have to need any mediatory source. Because truth, in view of Gandhi itself is God, but accepting relative truth as secondary reality, (like advaita vedanta) he seems to term God as the truth of the lower level. But from all the texts of Mahatma Gandhi, we find only one conclusion and that is, "Truth is God and God is truth." Thus Gandhi himself contradicts his own idea. This contradiction begets confusion in human mind. If Gandhi is advaitic in his view, a follower of Gandhism must have to believe in only one truth as ultimate reality, as the cause of creation. If he is vishishtadvaitic in his view, his follower must have to believe in God as creator of the universe. Accepting the advaitic trend of Gandhism, a man must have the conclusion that the whole universe is unreal. Real is only truth. This conclusion impliese that there is no moral or immoral action as such. Truth is only reality and the whole universe is its manifestation. Truth as ultimate reality is beyond morality, it means that every action of human being are legalised in the society. Perhapes, it is the cause that our society in recent times is full of social evils like bribery, corruption, rape, murder, decoity, dishonesty, lieness etc. This is nothing but the negative impact of truth as an element of *Satyagraha*.

Accepting the vishishtadvaitic trend of Gandhian thought, we may have the concluation that the whole world is as real as its prime cause, God. God is pure, love, kind, noble, meek etc. So, His manifestation (i.e. the world) must be the same. But what we experience is not the same. The world is full of sufferings, pains etc. It is worst effect of God. So it contradicts the noble nature of God. This contradiction leads us to assume that God is not the creater of our universe. So what a man does either good or bad, in moral sense, he is the sole responsible for this. So, Gandhi's claim of "man's actions depends upon himself but the result of action depends upon God", is in vain. If this claim has to be accepted, it means that man should act without thinking the result of his action. Such action leads the society towards the chaotic situation as we feel now-a-days. This is also the negative implication of Gandhian view of truth as an elements of *Satyagraha*.

Knowladge is a process of knowing the truth. Truth is an object and process and object are different in nature. But Gandhi does not understand this difference and he assimilates truth and knowledge together. This is his fault which leads the conclusion that object is process and process is object. In other words, there is no knowladge but truth itself only. It implise that every member of the society is without knowledge and thus all are ignorant. Ignorant is never bliss but course. In real sense after nearly five decades of independence of our country, our fellow beings are even ignorent. In fact, our rulers who claims to be Gandhian or followers of Gandhian ideology are absolutely responsible for making the pepole of free India ignorent, as the only want their votes. If our pepole is educated, rules cannot be successful to get votes of the ignorent and illiterate Indians. Most of Indian people are uneducated and they are being exploited on the ground of their equal participation in making the government. This is also one of the negative implication of Gandhian Satyagraha in its form of truth.

Truthfulness is a moral act which is identified with truth by Gandhi. Morality is mobile but truth as metaphysical entity is immobile. Mobility and immobility are not the same. But Gandhi has attempted to assimilate both opposite natured being which is quite impossible. Secondly, it is also impossible to speak truth always. Gandhi also feels it, and therefore he says that one should speak truth with sweet tongue because harsh truth has not been sanctioned by Gandhi. But in fact whatever is true is always harsh. Perhapes Gandhi forgets this fact and adopted liberal attitude which also impacts the society negetively. If a man does not speak harsh truth, it means he is unable to speak real truth. In other words, Gandhi inspires his fellow being to speak impure truth or the mixture of both truth and falsity. This happens an our society now-a-days. All of our political and social leaders, reformer including the rules are in habit speak truth with falsity, and so our people too. This leads to the present situation of chaotic and instable society in which we live. Thus truth as an element of *Satyagraha* negatively affects our society.

After truth, non-violance is the second important element of Satyagraha. Non-violance is non-injury, non-killing in speech, thought and action. However, Gandhi is also liberal in adopting non-violance as an element of Satyagraha, when he has sanctioned to kill the ill calf. It is his liberal attitude of accepting non-violance. Killing calf either illed or non-illed is not non-violance act. Thus Gandhi once again has confused moral and immoral act together. This confusion creates human society corrupt, instable and disordered because each and every man gets freedom to make harm to someone to whom he desire, only after proving that very man ill, and dangerous for our society. So far as proving ill or dangerous is concerned, We have found that in present corrupt soceity it is possible with helf of lieness and bribery. It is also the negative implication of non-violance as an element of Satyagraha.

The implication of Swadeshi as an element of satyagraha in our society is also negative one. Swadeshi has two aspects-nationalism and internationalism. The word "swadeshi" projects nationalism, but Gandhi's liberal attitude indicates that swadeshi is not so narrow that it should be confind with nationalism. Therefore, Gandhi's view on Swadeshi implise internationalism too. Today, each and every Indian with a few exception are surrounded with international culture. Indian (or nation) culture is absolutely different form international one. Nationalism implise patriotism, but internationalism inspires human being (especially Indians) to be westernised. Most of our pepole are swinging in naked culture of the west. This leads human society into nudeness, corruption and other kinds of immoral acts. Thus, all elements of Satyagraha leads human socity, particularly Indian, into corruption and disorder.

Satyagraha, as Gandhi uses, it is a peaceful non-violance movement to fulfil one's own ends in the interest of the society. But what records of this movement we have, it proves that this is not a peaceful and non-violent movement rather violent and choatic one. The best example of Gandhi's unsuccessful Satyagraha movement is "Chauri Chaura" incident. Non-cooperation, civil disobedience and fasting are forms of Satyagraha. As we have already seen that all these forms are in fact fallacious, and they affect society in wrong direction. Civil disobedience is a violation of state-laws. Every citizen should have to obey state-law, but by civil disobedience a citizen learns to be undutiful. Gandhi has used civil disobedience a citizen learns to be undutiful. Gandhi has used civil disobedience in the special circumstances. But today the circumstances is changed. So civil disobedience is an out dated resort of Satyagraha movement. Now its pious aim has been turned into selfish end. This is the same case with non-cooperation. Therefore, Satyagraha inspires human beings to be egoist. Strike, a simple technique of Satyagraha was adopted by Gandhi to make protest against the injustices and corrupt rule of the British. He used it in course of freedom struggle to make mass people active for the enforcement of social and political demands. But now-a-day strike has became the simplest weapon to achieve the personal or collective desire of the working class. Fasting is also a negative approach of Satyagraha. Gandhi uses fasting as a political means, but it is in fact a religious one. Politics and religion are not the same. However,

Publishing House, Ahmedabad, 1951.

Satyagraha: Non-violent Resistance (1910-1935), Navajivan Publishing House, Ahmedabad, 1951.

Satyagraha in South Africa, Translated from the Gujarati by Desai, V. G., Navajivan Publishing House, Ahmedabad, 1950.

Socialism of My Conception, Edited by Hingorani, T. Anand, Bharatiya Vidya Bhawan, Bombay, 1957.

Selection from Gandhi, Edited by Bose, N.K., Navajivan Publishing House, Ahmedabad, 1957.

Self-restraint vs. Self-indulgence, Navajivan Publishing House, Ahmedabad, 1958.

Speeches and Writing of Mahatma Gandhi, G. A. Natesan and Co., Madras, 1922.

Swadeshi : True or False, Harijan Office, Poona, 1939.

Swaraj Through Charkha, All India Spinners' Association, Sevagram, Wardha, 1945.

The Removal of Untouchability, Navajivan Publishing House, Ahmedabad,1954.

The Collected Works of Mahatma Gandhi, 35 vols., The Publication Division, Goverment of India, New Delhi.

The Teachings of Mahatma Gandhi, Edited by Chander, J.P., The Indian Printing Works, Lahore, 1945.

The Thought of Mahatma Gandhi : A Digest, Complied by Mirabegu, Navajivan Publishing House, Ahmedabad, 1962.

The Mind of Mahatma Gandhi, (Editors) Prabhu, R.K. and Rao U.R. Navjivan Publishing House, Ahmedabad, 1969.

Trusteeship, Compiled and edited by Kelekar, Ravindra, Navjivan Publishing House, Ahmedabad, 1960.

Towards Lasting Peace, edited by Hingorani, T. Anand, Bharatiya Vidya Bhawan, Bombay, 1956.

Towards Non-Violent Socialism, edited by Kumarappa, Bharatan, Navjivan Publishing House, Ahmedabad, 1951.

Truth is God, Compiled by Prabhu, R. K., Navajivan Publishing House, Ahmedabad, 1955.

Village Swaraj, Complied by Vyas, H. M., Navajivan Publishing House, Ahmedabad, 1962.

Varnashrama Dharma, Complied by Prabhu, R. K. , Navajivan Publishing House, Ahmedabad, 1962.

Wit and Wisdom of Gandhi, edited by Jack, H. A., Beacon Press, Boston, 1951.

B. Periodicals

Harijan (English Weekly), 1933-41, Poona; 1942, 1946-48, Ahmedabad.

Indian Opinion (English Weekly), 1903-14, Phoenix, Natal *Young India* (English Weekly), 1919-32, Ahmedabad.

Other Authors' Writings on Mahatma Gandhi and his ideas

A. BOOKS

Alexander, Horace, G. *et. al., Social and Political Ideas of World*, Gandhi, Indian Council of World Affairs, New Delhi, 1949.

Andrews, C. F., *Mahatma Gandhi's Ideas*, Allen and Anwin, London, 1929.

Azad, Abul Kalam, *India Wins Freedom*, Orient Longman, Bombay, 1959.

Adhikari, G., *Gandhism A Review*, Bombay 1940.

Appadorai, A., *Documents in Political Thought in Modern India*, Oxford University Press, Delhi, 1981.

Birla, G. D., *In The Shadow of Mahatma*, Orient Longmans, Bombay, 1953.

Bhagwandas, Babu, *The Philosophy of Non-cooperation*, Tagore and Co., Madras, 1922.

Bhave, Vinoba. *Swaraj Shastra : Principles, Non-Violent Political order*, Akhila Bharat Sarva Seva Sangh Prakashan, Varanasi, 1963.

Bhave, Viñoba. *Gram Swaraj our Birthright*, Sarvodya Prachūralay, Thanjavur, India of Serva Seva Sangh Prakashan, Varanasi, 1966.

Bondurent, Joan V., *Conquest of Violence*, Oxford University, Press Bombay, 1959.

Bose, N. K., *Studies in Gandhism*, Indian Associated Publishing Co., Calcutta, 1947.

Biswas, S. C. Gandhi: *Theory and Practice: Social Impact and Comtemporary Relevance* (Proceedings of Seminar), Indian Institute of Advanced Study, Simla, 1969.

Belton, G., *The Tragedy of Gandhi*, London, 1934.

Birla, G. D., *Bapu* (Hindi) Delhi, 1944.

Barr, F. Marry, *Conversations and Correspondance with Mahatma Gandhi*, Bombay, 1945.

Basu, N., *Political Philosophy after Hegel and Marx*, Grantha Bhawan, Calcutta, 1956.

Bhattacharya, B. D., *Evolutions of The Political Philosophy of Mahatma Gandhi*, Calcutta Book House, 1969.

Chaudhary, P. G. Roy, *Gandhiji's First Struggle in India*, Navajivan Publishing House, Ahmedabad, 1955.

Coker, F.W., *Recent Political Thought*, The World Press, 1957.

Dhawan, G. N., *The Political Philosophy of Mahatma Gandhi*, Navajivan Publishing House, Ahmedabad, 1957.

Diwakar, R. R., *Satyagraha : The Pathway to Peace*, Pustak Bhandar Patna, 1950.

Diwakar, R. R., *Satyagraha : Its Technique and History*, Hind Kitabs, Bombay, 1946.

Diwakar, R. R., *Gandhi's Triple Massage*, Bhartiya Vidya Bhawan, Chowpattey, Bombay, 1966.

Datta, D.M., *The Philosophy of Mahatma Gandhi*, University of Wisconsin Press, Madison, 1953 & University of Calcutta, 1968.

Dantwala, M. L., *Gandhism Reconsidered*, Padma Publications, Bombay, 1944.

Dharmamadhikari, Dada, *Ahimsak Kranti Ki Prakriya* (Hindi), A. B. Sarva Seva Sangh, Kashi, 1962.

Despande, P. G., *Gandhian: A Bibliography of Gandhian Literature*, Navajivan Publishing House,Ahmedabad, 1948.

Doctor, A. H., *Anarchist Throught in India*, Asia Publishing House, Bombay, 1964.

Doctor, J. J., *M. K., Gandhi : An Indian Patriot in South Africa*, Publications Division, Ministry of Informantion and Broadcasting, Goverment of India, 1967.

Doke, J. J., *Gandhi : An Indian Patriot*, Madras,1909.

Elwip, Verrier, *Religious and Culture Aspects of Khadhi*, Sarvodaya Prachwalaya, Thanjavur, 1964.

Fisher, Louis, *The Life of Mahatma Gandhi*, Harper and Bros, New York, 1950.

Gregg, R. B., *The Power of Non-Violance*, Navajivan Publishing, House, Ahmedabad, 1960.

Gregg, R. B., *A Dicipline For Non-Violance*, Navajivan Publishing House, Ahmedabad, 1941.

George, S. K., *Gandhi's Challenge to Christianity: An Essay in Appreciation*, Ahmedabad, 1941.

Guenon, Rane, *An Introduction to the Study of Hindu Doctrine*, London, 1945.

Gupta, N. N., *Gandhi and Gandhism*, Hind Kitabs, Bombay, 1984.

Gray, R. M. & Parekh, M. C., *Mahatma Gandhi*, Calcutta, 1953.

Galloway, G., *The Philosophy of Religion*, The Volume of International and Theological Liberary, New York.

Holmes, J.H., *Gandhi : The Christ of Today*. Tagore and Co., Madras, 1922.

Holmes, J. H., *My Gandhi*, Allen and Unwin, London, 1554.

Jaju, Shri Krishnadas, *The Ideology of the Charkha*, Akhil Bharat Sarva Seva Sangh, Kashi, 1958.

Jha, S. N., *A Critical Study of Gandhian Economic Thought*, Agra, Lakshmi Narain Agrawal, 1961.

Joshi, L. *Sastri, A Critic of Hinduism.*

Kalelkar, Kaka, *Gandhibad Samajvad* (Hindi) Sasta Sahitya Mandal, New Delhi, 1939.

Kripalani, J. B., *Class Struggle*, Akhil Bharat Serva Seva Sangh Prakashan, Rajghat, Kashi, 1958.

Kripalani, J. B., *Politics of Charakha*, Vora and Co., Bombay, 1946.

Kripalani, J.B., *Gandhi : His Life and Thought*, Publications Division, Ministry of Informantion and Broadcasting, Government of India, 1970.

Kumarappa, J. C., *Gandhian Economic Thought*, Akhil Bharat Sarva Seva Sangh Prakashan, Rajghat, Varanasi, 1962.

Kumarappa, J. C., *The Gandhian Way of Life*, All India Village Industries Association, Wardha, 1952.

Kumarappa, J. C., *Swaraj for the Masses*, Akhil Bharat Serva Seva Sangh Prakashan, Kashi, 1958.

Krishnamurti, Y, G., *Gandhism in the Atomic Age*, Shakti Karyalayam, Madras, 1947.

Krishnamaruti, Y. G., *Gandhism will Survive*, Pustak Bhandar, Patna 1949.

Kripalani, J. B., *The Gandhian Way*. Bombay, 1938.

Kripalani, K. R., *Gandhi, Tagore and Nehru*, Bombay 1947.

Kosambi, Dharmanand, *Bhartiya Sanskriti our Ahimsa*, Bombay, 1948.

Krishna Das, *Seven Months with Mahatma Gandhi* I and II Volumes, Madras 1928.

Lohia, Ram Manohar, *Marx, Gandhi and Sociolism*, Neva Hind Publication, Hyderabad, 1963.

Lenin, V. I., *State and Revolution*, Foreign Languages Publishing House, Moscow, 1953.

Ligt, De Bart, *The Conquest of Violance: An Eassy on War and Revolution*, George Routledge and Sons, London, 1937.

Lovett, Sir V., *A History of Indian National Movement.*

Lal, B. K., *Indian Philosophy*, Moti Lal Banarsidas, Patna.

Lal, B. K., *Contemporary Indian Philosophy*, Moti Lal Banarsidas, Patna.

Manubahen, Gandhi, *The End of an Epoch*, Translated from Gujarati by Gandhi, Gopal Krishna, Navjivan Publishing House, Ahmedabad, 1962.

Mathur, J. S., *Essays on Gandhian Economics*, Chaitanya Publishing House, Allahabad, 1959.

Mallick, Gurdial., *Gandhi and Tagore*, Navajivan Publishing House, Ahmedabad, 1961.

Mukherjee, Hiren, *Gandhij; A Study*, Pepole's Publishing House, Calcutta, 1958.

Majumdar, B. B., *Gandhian Concept of State*, M. G., Sarkar & Sons, Calcutta, 1957.

Mashruwala, K. G., *Practical Non-Violance*, Navajivan Publishing House, Ahmedabad, 1958.

Mashruwala, K. G., *Gandhi and Marx*, Navajivan Publishing House, Ahmedabad, 1953 .

Namboodaripad, E. M. S., *The Mahatma and The Ism*, People's Publishing House, New Delhi, 1959.

Nag, Kalidas, *Tolstoy and Gandhi*, Pustak Bhandar, Patna 1950.

Nanda, B.R., *Mahatma Gandhi : A Biography*, Allen and Unwin, London, 1958.

Nehru, Jawaharlal, *Mahatma Gandhi*, Singel Press, Calcutta, 1949.

Narayan, J. P., *From Socialism to Sarvodaya*, Akhil Bharat Serva Seva Sangh Prakashan, Rajghat, Kashi, 1959.

Narayan, J. P., *Towards a New Society*, New Delhi, 1958.

Natesan, G. A., *Gandhi : The Tan and His Mission*, Madras, 1932.

Osho, R., *Dekh Kabira Roya*, Rajnesh Foundation Ltd. Swami Yoga Pratap Bharati.

Polak, H. S. L., *Mahatma Gandhi*, Madras, 1930.

Polak, M. G., *Mr. Gandhi*, The Man, London, 1931.

Patwardhan, Appa, *Towards a New Society*, Akhil Bharat Sarva Seva Sangh, Kashi, 1959.

Prasad, Mahadeva, *Social Philosophy of Mahatma Gandhi*, Vishwavidyalaya Prakashan, Gorakhpur, 1958.

Prasad, Rajendra, *Satyagraha in Champaran*, Navajivan Publshing House, Ahmedabad, 1949.

Pyarelal, *Gandhian Techniques in The Modern World*, Navajivan Publishing House, Ahmedabad, 1969.

Pyarelal, *Towards New Horizons*, Navajivan Publishing House,

Ahmedabad, 1959.

Pyarelal, *Mahatma Gandhi : Early Phase*, Vol. I, Navajivan Publishing House, Ahmedabad, 1965.

Pyarelal, *Mahatma Gandhi : The Last Phase*, 2 vols, Navajivan Publishing House, Ahmedabad, 1966 & 1967.

Pyarelal, *A Pilgrimage for Peace*, Navajivan Publishing House, Ahmedabad 1950.

Prasad, R. C., *Acharya Rajnesh and Kamayoga*, Dharma our Gandhi, Patna.

Prabhavananda, S., *Vedic Religion and Philosophy*, Sri Ramakrishna Math, Madras, 1983.

Patil, Dr. S.H., *Gandhi and Swaraj*, Deep and Deep Publications, New Delhi, 1983.

Pal, B. C., *The Spiritt of Indian Nationalism.*

Radhakrishnan, S., *Mahatma Gandhi: Essays and Reflections on his life and work*, Allen and Unwin, London, 1959.

Roy, Benoy Goal, *Gandhian Ethics*, Navajivan Publishing House Ahmedabad, 1958.

Rao, M. B., *The Mahatma : A Marxist Symposium*, Pepole's Publishing House, New Delhi, 1969.

Russell, B., *Principles of Social Reconstruction*, London, 1950.

Rolland, Romain, *Mahatma Gandhi,* Century & Co., London,1924.

Ruthnaswamy, M., *The Political Philosophy of Mr. Gandhi,*Tagore & Co., Madras, 1922.

Roy, M.N., *One Year of Non-Cooperation*, Calcutta, 1923.

Roy, M. N., *The Aftermath of non-Cooperation*, London, 1926.

Roy, M. N., *Gandhism, Nationalism and Socialism*, New York, 1940.

Roy, M. N., *Letters to Mahatma*, New York 1940.

Roy, M. N., *Reason, Romanticism and Revoluation*, New York, 1952.

Sharma, B. S., *Gandhi as a Political Thinker*, Indian Press, Allahabad,1956.

Sharma, S. R., *The Man and the Mahatma*, Rajan, Chandigarh, 1985.

Swarupananda, S., *Shrimad Bhagvad Gita*, Advaita Ashrama, Calcutta, 1982.

Sexena, Kiran, *Modern Indian Political Thought*, Chetna Publications, New Delhi, 1978.

Sharma, D. S., *A Primer of Hinduism*, Shri Ramakrishna Math, Madras

Stent, D., *Religious Studies*, Heineman, London, 1983.

Singh, Dr. *Ramjee, Gandhi Darshan Mimasa*, Bihar Hindi Granth Acadamy, Patna, 1973.

Santhanam, K., *Satyagraha and State*, Bombay, 1960.

Shukla Chandrashekhar, *Gandhi's View of life*, Bhartiya Vidya Bhawan, Chowpatty, Bombay, 1952.

Spratt, P., *Gandhism : An Analysis*, Madras, 1939.

Thoreau, H. D., *Civil Disobedience*, S. Genesan, Madras, 1922.

Tandon, Vishwanath, *The Social and Political Philosophy of Sarvodaya After Gandhi*, Sarva Seva Sangh Prakashan, Rajghat, Varanasi, 1965.

Tendulkar, D. G., *Mahatma—The Life of Mohandas Karamchand Gandhi*, 8 vols, Publications Division, Government of India, New Delhi, 1960-61

Unnithan, T. K. N., *Gandhi and Free India : J. B. Wolters*, Groningen, 1956.

Verma, V. P., *The Political Philosophy of Mahatma Gandhi and Sarvodaya*, Lakshmi Narayan Agrawal, Agra, 1959.

B. Periodicals & Newspapers

Amrit Bazar Patrika, Calcutta.
The Modern Review, Calcutta.
Gandhi Marg, New Delhi.
Gram Udyog Patrika, Wardha.
Khadigramodyog, Bombay.
Sarvodaya, Tanjore.

C. Sanskrit Text and Translations

Vedas (All four)
Upnisads (Isavasyopanished, Tatriyopanishad, etc.)
Puranas (Vishnupuran)
Manu Smriti
Ramayna (Valmiki & Tulsi)
Mahabharata
Bhagvad Gita
Shankar Bharhmasutrabhasya
Sarva Darshan Samgraha

INDEX